Disconnecting Bell
The Impact of the AT&T Divestiture

Edited by
Harry M. Shooshan III
Institute for Information Policy

PERGAMON PRESS

New York Oxford Toronto Sydney Paris Frankfurt

Pergamon Press Offices:

U.S.A.   Pergamon Press Inc., Maxwell House, Fairview Park,
                     Elmsford, New York 10523, U.S.A.

U.K.   Pergamon Press Ltd., Headington Hill Hall,
                     Oxford OX3 0BW, England

CANADA   Pergamon Press Canada Ltd., Suite 104, 150 Consumers Road,
                     Willowdale, Ontario M2J 1P9, Canada

AUSTRALIA   Pergamon Press (Aust.) Pty. Ltd., P.O. Box 544,
                     Potts Point, NSW 2011, Australia

FRANCE   Pergamon Press SARL, 24 rue des Ecoles,
                     75240 Paris, Cedex 05, France

FEDERAL REPUBLIC Pergamon Press GmbH, Hammerweg 6,
OF GERMANY   D-6242 Kronberg-Taunus, Federal Republic of Germany

Library of Congress Cataloging in Publication Data
Main entry under title:

Disconnecting Bell.

        Includes bibliographical references and index.
        1. American Telephone and Telegraph Company.
2. Telephone--Law and legislation--United States.
3. Telecommunication--Law and legislation--United States.
4. Corporate divestiture--United States. I. Shooshan,
Harry M.
KF2849.A4D57   1984   384.6'065'73   83-25053
ISBN 0-08-030173-8
ISBN 0-08-030172-X (pbk.)

Printed in the United States of America

Dedicated to
Ithiel de Sola Pool
1917-1984
All of us have been challenged by his
ideas, and many of us were touched by
his personality and probing mind. We are
honored to share this book with him.

—The Editor and Contributors

CONTENTS

PREFACE

Over the course of this century, what has come to be known as the Bell System has played a quiet but pervasive role in the lives of virtually all Americans. Yet, until January 8, 1982, few understood how the American Telephone and Telegraph Company, or AT&T, had developed, how it had almost single-handedly constructed the world's largest and most successful telecommunications network, or why the federal government fought long and hard to dismantle one of the most efficient business enterprises ever assembled.

While the resolve of the U.S. Department of Justice never wavered through the administrations of three presidents, its task to break up the Bell monopoly and open the communications marketplace to competitive forces was not an easy one. For in its decision to end AT&T's monopoly, it was taking on a corporate kingdom of three million investors, over one million employees with an annual payroll exceeding $21 billion, and assets worth more than those of General Motors, Ford, Chrysler, General Electric, and IBM *combined*.

Yet, on January 8, AT&T and the Justice Department announced agreement on a 19-page document which, with some modification, has become not only the blueprint for the largest corporate divestiture in U.S. history, but also the foundation for the future development of the telecommunications industry. On that date, Bell agreed to end its control of 22 local operating companies, comprising the bulk of the traditional telephone industry, in exchange for an end to a prohibition on entry into the unregulated telecommunications marketplace.

The event was momentous for a number of reasons. Among them is that the breakup occurred at a time when the political trends of the nation had taken a decidedly deregulatory turn. Additionally, the 1982 consent decree more than any other single event heralds an era of dramatic change in our standard of living brought on primarily by emerging competing forces and rapid advances in communications technology.

Why was the Bell breakup necessary? What were the forces which led to the historic announcement of January 8, 1982? How will AT&T and the divested operating companies do business in the coming years? How will their competitors bring new products and services to the new marketplace?

And, finally, what impact will the antitrust settlement have on our lives?

These are some of the questions which have occupied the time and attention of communications leaders, scholars, lawyers, economists, regulators, and politicians for much of the past two years. To help focus attention on these questions and to assist the public in understanding the role of communications in our lives, the Institute for Information Policy and the Aspen Institute for Humanistic Studies have selected a group of telecommunications experts to write the collection of essays which comprise this book.

Both organizations are actively involved in focusing attention on changes taking place in telecommunications policy. Founded in 1982, the Institute for Information Policy studies and fosters the development of a coherent policy governing information transfer in the United States. The Institute is planning a series of conferences and seminars designed to bring together a wide range of representatives from the academic and professional fields to debate and exchange ideas on new developments in the communications and information spheres.

The Aspen Institute for Humanistic Studies, formed in 1949, brings together leaders from all pursuits in a continuing series of conferences and seminars to help educate Americans on major issues of public concern.

The latest of these meetings was cohosted by the Institute for Information Policy and the Aspen Institute. Held on the Aspen Institute's Wye Plantation on the eastern shore of Maryland in June 1983, the two-day workshop was attended by authors of the essays in this book as well as a panel of communications experts. The workshop critiqued and debated the points discussed in drafts of each chapter. Many of the points and issues raised during this meeting were incorporated in the essays which appear in this book.

We are grateful for the support and enthusiasm the Wye Plantation meeting generated. To the following attendees, our deepest thanks:

Raymond M. Alden, United Telecommunications, Inc.
Merrill Brown, *The Washington Post*
Robert W. Crandall, Brookings Institution
Lee S. Cutliff, AT&T
Gary M. Epstein, Federal Communications Commission
Henry Geller, Washington Center for Public Policy Research
Linda Grant, *Los Angeles Times*
Winston Himsworth, Lehman Bros.
Charles L. Jackson, Shooshan & Jackson Inc.
Konrad Kalba, Kalba Bowen Associates, Inc.
Jill Kasle, Center for Telecommunications Studies, George Washington University
Robert E. LaBlanc, Robert E. LaBlanc Associates, Inc.
Susan W. Leisner, Florida Public Service Commission
William McGowan, MCI Communications
Roger Noll, California Institute of Technology
Bruce M. Owen, Owen, Greenhalgh & Myslinski

Michael Pertschuk, Federal Trade Commission
Ithiel de Sola Pool, Massachusetts Institute of Technology
Harvey L. Poppel, Booz Allen & Hamilton, Inc.
Jeffrey H. Rohlfs, Shooshan & Jackson Inc.
Richard E. Wiley, Wiley, Johnson & Rein
Charles Zielinski, Wald, Harkrader & Ross

The editors of this book also wish to thank others who contributed to its preparation, including Mary Ann Castillo who coordinated the project in Washington and made it possible for the manuscripts to be transmitted directly from disc which greatly reduced production time, and Patricia Kinaga who assisted in these efforts. We also want to thank the people from Pergamon Press—David Kellogg, Lynn Rosen, and Jerry Frank—for their guidance. We appreciate the research assistance provided by the Center for Telecommunications Studies and by James R. Patton.

Grateful acknowledgement is given to the John and Mary R. Markle Foundation for the grant which made this project possible in the first place. Special thanks go to Mary Milton of the Markle Foundation and to Michael Rice of the Aspen Institute for their support and encouragement.

We are especially grateful to Charles L. Brown, Chairman of AT&T, for taking the time and interest to contribute his personal views on the restructuring of his company which serve as the introduction to this volume.

The book consists of nine separate essays by leading experts, most of whom have also been active participants in the events leading up to the breakup of the Bell System. Chip Shooshan has written a chapter which sets the stage for the breakup and identifies the major forces that contributed to this unprecedented corporate restructuring. Dick Wiley explains how the policy of competition forced change on the Bell System.

The implications of the divestiture for economic theory are explored by noted economists Bob Crandall and Bruce Owen. The impact of the new structure on technology, in general, and on Bell Laboratories, in particular, is discussed by Chuck Jackson.

The problems presented by the breakup for policymakers and regulators on the federal and state levels are examined by Henry Geller and Chuck Zielinski.

Ithiel de Sola Pool and Linda Grant provide somewhat different assessments of the divestiture and of the extent to which society will benefit from it.

Taken together, these chapters provide interesting insights and raise many provocative questions that are certain to dominate the discussions of this event in months to come.

Harry M. Shooshan, III
Arthur M. Hill, II

Disconnecting Bell

THE BELL SYSTEM: OLD AND NEW

NYNEX
New England Telephone
New York Telephone

Bell Atlantic
New Jersey Bell
Bell of Pennsylvania
Diamond State Telephone
C&P Telephone

Bell South
Southern Bell
South Central Bell

Ameritech
Michigan Bell
Ohio Bell
Indiana Bell
Illinois Bell
Wisconsin Telephone

Southwestern Bell
Southwestern Bell

U S West
Northwestern Bell
Mountain States
Pacific Northwest Bell
Nevada Bell

Pacific Telesis
Pacific Telephone

1
A PERSONAL INTRODUCTION

by Charles L. Brown
Chairman of the Board,
American Telephone & Telegraph

Among the sweeping changes in U.S. telecommunications in the 1980s, probably no single development loomed larger than the decision by AT&T to accept the Justice Department's proposal to break up the Bell System.

For many years to come, the rationale and results of AT&T's decision to accept divestiture will undoubtedly be analyzed and debated by historians, in business schools, and by other observers of the public policy process in America.

My intention here is not to debate or defend that decision, but rather to describe from my perspective the process that, over a number of years, led to this historic event, and to discuss some of its implications for the future.

I think it is important to understand that our decision to accept such a radical restructuring of our business was not a spur-of-the-moment action. Admittedly, it caught many people by surprise. Unquestionably, it represented a reversal of a position we had advocated, vigorously and continuously, for decades. Clearly, it represented the most significant discontinuity in the history of this enterprise.

However, in my view, it did not represent a significant discontinuity in the basic philosophy that has guided this business for most of its history. That philosophy, first stated by the organizational patriarch of the Bell System, Theodore Vail, is that the major task of management is to conform the business to the desires of the public.

This notion was based on the conviction that no business—particularly one charged with providing such a vital public service as communications— can exist without public permission nor long succeed without public approval.

It was that philosophy which led Vail, at the beginning of this century, to embrace regulation as a substitute for competition, so as to permit the orderly development of an efficient nationwide communications system. And it was the same philosophy that led me, three-quarters of a century later, to embrace competition as a substitute for regulation—this time in response to the public's desire for diversity in communications services and suppliers.

Thus, our decision in January 1982 to accept the Justice Department's divestiture proposal did not reflect a change in philosophy, but a change in circumstances. Our decision to divest was, in reality, a decision to adapt our organization to the changed expectations of the American public. Or rather, I should say to the expectations of the public's representatives in various branches of government.

Our decision to accept divestiture was rooted in developments going back to the 1960s, when the Federal Communications Commission began making a series of decisions aimed at introducing competition in selected parts of the telecommunications market. The first of these focused on the provision of customer premises equipment, such as telephones and PBXs. These were followed by decisions permitting competition in point-to-point private line service and, eventually, through the courts, in regular long-distance service.

At first, AT&T's reaction was restrained and statesmanlike. But we did express concerns. Our initial reservations focused on the risks to service quality if all sorts of hardware could be attached to the telephone network. But as events unfolded, our principal concern was the impact of competition on the telephone industry's traditional rate structure. Over the years, this rate structure had incorporated social as well as economic objectives—for example, nationwide averaging of long-distance rates and using long-distance revenues to subsidize local telephone service.

We knew very well that while competition might benefit some users, it would ultimately mean higher prices and less convenience for other users, especially for the average home telephone customer. Although many people dismissed this concern at the time, that is exactly what began happening in the early 1980s. In 1984, nearly everyone understands it.

By 1973, it was becoming increasingly clear that the policy direction being taken by the FCC was irreversible. In response, we said that if there was to be competition, it should at least be full and fair competition, with the same ground rules for us as for everyone else.

Regrettably, that did not happen. Regrettably, every decision supposedly aimed at creating more competition produced more regulation—at least for AT&T.

We continued to be confronted with two sets of ground rules: one providing virtually unrestricted entry for our competitors, the other placing severe restrictions on our ability to compete back. Rather than true competition, we faced the worst of all worlds—regulated, contrived competition.

At that point, under the leadership of my predecessor, John deButts, we shifted from cautious statesmanship to vigorous spokesmanship. In every available forum, we tried to alert the public to the effects these policies would have on the cost and quality of service to the average telephone customer. We argued that before going further down this road, the public should have an opportunity to decide whether this was really the direction in which they wanted to go.

Sad to say, the only thing the general public decided was to ignore the whole thing. Since telephone service was good and inexpensive, it was hard to get people excited about such arcane subjects as nationwide average pricing.

Then, in 1974, the Department of Justice filed its massive antitrust suit, seeking nothing less than the full dismemberment of the Bell System.

In 1976, at the urging of AT&T and the independently-owned telephone companies, Congress began what was to become an annual effort to update national telecommunications policy, a policy framed in law back in 1934.

During this time, of course, the onward march of technology continued. This new technology—much of it from Bell Laboratories—was gradually but surely obliterating the traditional boundaries between communications and data processing.

However, AT&T continued to be saddled with a 1956 consent decree confining the Bell System to regulated telecommunications. Drafted in an earlier era, this decree had become an outdated, one-way passageway. Others could enter our business at will, but we could not stray beyond the confines of traditional telephony. We were, in effect, being deprived of the fruits of our own technology, our own innovation.

When I became chief executive officer of AT&T in 1979, one of the principal objectives I set for myself was to find a way out of this legal-legislative-regulatory quagmire.

Since a change in command provides an opportunity to open new avenues, I used that opportunity to signal our readiness to search for a new consensus on telecommunications policy, and our willingness—without preconceptions—to consider alternative futures.

In the months that followed, each branch of government tried independently to fashion a new structure for our industry.

The FCC's solution was embodied in the landmark decision it reached in the Second Computer Inquiry. Instead of trying to distinguish between telecommunications and data processing, this approach was to try to draw a bright line between Bell's provision of basic communications services and everything else.

Congress was studying a variety of legislative proposals that would restructure the industry and rewrite the existing statutes. But as is often the case, each house had a different solution.

Overshadowing all was the brooding spectre of the Justice Department case. In the course of time, all the other initiatives might prove moot, and the world's largest and, in many ways, most technically complicated business might be reorganized by lawyers.

Through all this, certain realities were becoming clear:

- Whatever happened in any of these arenas, the marketplace was to be the key instrument for governing the telecommunications industry in the years ahead. Competition would be the rule, not the exception.
- The Bell System was perceived in some quarters as too big, too powerful, too pervasive.
- Time was not in the Bell System's favor. Unless we could cut this Gordian knot—and soon—the market opportunities created by our own technology might pass us by.

It had become clear that to gain access to new markets—and, in fact, to retain access to our existing markets—the Bell System would have to agree to some form of structural change, most likely a radical restructuring.

After considerable study, we concluded that the antitrust issues needed to be resolved first. We had three options.

We could continue the litigation—a costly, distracting process that probably would not produce a final decision for years—and likely in the Supreme Court.

A second option was to settle the case by subjecting the Bell System to an elaborate injunctive decree that contained the restrictive provisions proposed in Congress, plus some additional provisions. There would be no divestiture, but the Bell System would be tied up by restrictions which, taken together, would outweigh the benefits of integration.

The third option was to consider the divestiture solution developed by the Justice Department—a solution that was drastic but not as Draconian as the one sought by the government at the onset of the case.

We chose the third option. We were confident we could ultimately disprove the government's contentions. But, we concluded that getting rid of the terrible uncertainty and capitalizing on future market opportunities were more important than vindicating our past behavior in a marketplace that no longer existed, and more important than preserving a corporate structure that would leave our future behavior continually vulnerable to antitrust attacks.

What's more, instead of insisting on demolishing the Bell System—as they had for years—the government's lawyers were proposing a remedy based on a coherent theory.

Their theory was to separate the Bell System's competitive operation from those they considered to be a natural monopoly. Their solution was for AT&T to separate its local exchange services from all its other operations, such as long-distance service, customer equipment, manufacturing and research.

It was a clean solution, but a painful one from our point of view. To retain vertical integration and gain the freedom to follow our technology into new markets, we would have to lay on the chopping block our well-functioning nationwide partnership of companies providing total, end-to-end communications service.

Yet, compared with the alternatives we faced at this particular juncture, there was much to be said in favor of this solution:

- It would recognize the basic incompatibility of monopoly and competition.
- It would defuse the issue of our alleged size and power.
- It should remove concerns about our using revenues from monopoly services to subsidize competitive offerings.
- It would remove the basis for our long-distance competitors' complaints about equal access to local networks.
- It would retain our ability to manage a nationwide network as a unified entity.
- It would preserve the vital link between our research and development unit and our manufacturing arm.
- It would remove the outmoded constraints of the 1956 Consent Decree and permit us to use our technology to the fullest in any market we chose.
- And by ending the antitrust suit, it would lift the cloud of uncertainty that had overshadowed our business for most of a decade—and threatened to do so for years to come.

In sum, it offered a comprehensive solution to a number of pressing concerns and, most important, an expeditious solution.

It was against this background that on January 8, 1982, we signed the Consent Decree in which we agreed to divest the local parts of our 22 principal operating telephone companies.

It was not a simple settlement, a fact made abundantly clear during the exhaustive court review process that followed and in the modifications required by the judge before approving the decree and the divestiture details.

At this writing we are in the final stages of divestiture. It is impossible to assess all the ramifications of the dissolution of the Bell System. Certainly, there have been costs beyond a dollars and cents calculation. One of the most regrettable ones for AT&T was the judge's determination that the Bell name should be assigned exclusively to the divested telephone companies. "Bell" had been part of AT&T's heritage from the beginning; giving it up was like giving up our birthright. But "AT&T," with a new symbol and logo, has quickly become comfortable and well-known.

Looking to the future, I have high expectations for both AT&T and the divested companies. The regional companies are starting off in sound financial condition, with an established base of customers, experienced management, skilled employees, and a high level of advanced technology. AT&T will be, in many respects, a new enterprise—an amalgam of our past strengths and our new capabilities focused in new ways on new opportunities, both domestic and abroad. The new AT&T will be a wholly competitive business in all its endeavors, even in the long-distance field where it, but not its competitors, remains under strict regulation.

Only time will tell whether or not the management of AT&T was right in its decision to accept divestiture and whether, or to what extent, the public will benefit from the breakup of the Bell System.

In any event, it is important to keep in mind that the restructuring of the Bell System is part of a changing national policy in telecommunications—the shift from reliance on regulation to reliance on the marketplace and competition.

Breaking up the Bell System may have resolved many of the problems of transforming a regulated monopoly into a competitive industry. But major policy issues remain, including the continuing role of regulation and the need to review those aspects of regulation that apply to us but not to our competitors.

In addition, the political temptation is strong to intervene in the process of removing cross-subsidies and driving prices toward costs, as must be done in a competitive environment. Political "solutions" are appearing to "solve" perceived economic problems of an electorate which is seeing price dislocations. It is not yet clear whether the U.S., having opted for competition, is to get political cold feet and interfere with its implementation.

Having opted for competition and reshaping the industry to that end, we need policies that recognize the realities and the dynamics of the telecommunications marketplace. If the nation is to reap the full benefits of competition, we need even-handed rules—not excessive regulations and restraints. I say this not to plead for immediate or all-out deregulation, but rather to suggest that it makes sense to remove, over time, unnecessary regulation. Let the market work.

Beyond the question of a fair and level competitive playing field in telecommunications, there are larger issues involving the vitality of the U.S. economy.

Telecommunications, or more broadly the information-handling industry, holds the key to solving some of the most fundamental economic problems facing the nation. For in the kind of society we live in today, and even more so in the future, communications and information handling are a component of virtually every other form of economic activity.

The industry has been called an enabling industry—enabling other industries to lower their costs, enhance their productivity, and expand their range of new opportunities. If this industry is efficient, innovative and responsive, its net impact will be felt throughout the nation's economy. It will help establish and maintain America's technological leadership and its ability to be competitive with its international rivals. There are plenty of examples in the world where the lack of this important infrastructure has held back economic progress.

America has embarked on a unique experiment in competitive communications. In many ways, one can say we have stumbled into it without the authority of thoughtful legislation and in the adversarial pressure cooker of legal, legislative and regulatory struggles. Bell System people intend to do their best to make the new world work, and it will need the good will of many others as well.

2
THE BELL BREAKUP

Putting It In Perspective

by Harry M. Shooshan, III

However you measured it, AT&T was big. With assets of nearly $150 billion, more than three million shareholders, and over a million employees, the American Telephone & Telegraph Company had been the driving force in tying Americans together with a communications network that is unparalleled in the world. Despite its size and pervasiveness, most people have come to take the telephone company for granted. When workers went on strike last summer, telephone service continued largely uninterrupted because so much of the network has been automated.

Yet, as the communications marketplace has changed, driven by new technology and the introduction of competition, the preoccupation with AT&T's size increased. This preoccupation, coupled with a series of attempts by the Bell System to destroy or delay competition, created a certain inevitability. In a sense, AT&T's size and dominance of all phases of the telecommunications marketplace could no longer be tolerated. And regulation—at the federal and state levels—would no longer be adequate, if it indeed ever was, to deal with the enormity of the Bell System. Something had to give.

On January 8, 1982, in two federal courtrooms several hundred miles apart, lawyers for the Department of Justice and AT&T set in motion a legal process which profoundly changed the Bell System. And in changing the Bell System, it has affected the lives of nearly every person in the United States.

The restructuring of Bell which took place on January 1, 1984, restructured a telephone system that is the backbone of a communications network that ties together nearly every business and every home in the United States. This book examines the impact of that restructuring from a number of different perspectives. Most importantly, the book assesses the future. How will the breakup of Bell change the economy, the nature of regulation, the services available to consumers, and the position of the United States in the world telecommunications marketplace?

But before looking ahead, it is useful to put all of this change into the proper context. And to do that, we have to look back almost to the beginning of the Bell System itself. The structure of the Bell System—and government efforts to deal with what were viewed as the anticompetitive elements of that structure—have been the source of controversy for the better part of this century.

The American Telephone and Telegraph Company was formally established on February 28, 1885. As a subsidiary of the American Bell Telephone Company, AT&T was to operate long-distance telephone lines to interconnect local exchange areas of the Bell companies. The certificate of incorporation filed with the State of New York gave only a hint of what the new company was to become. The company was being formed "for the purpose of constructing, buying, owning, leasing, or otherwise obtaining lines of electric telegraph partly within and partly beyond the limits of the State of New York. . . ." Although it seemed almost incomprehensible in 1885, the plan was to extend those "electric telegraph" lines to connect "each and every city, town, or place in the State of New York with one or more points in each and every other city, town, or place in said state, and each and every other of the United States, and in Canada and Mexico . . . and by cable and other appropriate means with the rest of the known world. . . ."

The first president of AT&T was Theodore N. Vail, who had been general manager of American Bell and chief of the United States Railway Mail Service.[1] At the time, AT&T's capital stock was valued at $100,000, and there were 1,000 shares divided among four shareholders.

In 1900, the corporate structure changed, and AT&T was transformed into a holding company which continued to operate the long-distance network but which was also the parent company of the Bell System. AT&T now owned the Western Electric Company which had been purchased in 1881 and had become the exclusive manufacturing arm of the Bell System.[2] With the incorporation of the Bell Telephone Laboratories in 1924, owned jointly by AT&T and Western Electric, the structure of the Bell System as we know it today was largely in place. One observer of the evolution of the Bell System described the AT&T of this period:

It is a large business with multitudinous activities, many of which are absolute necessities of modern existence. It serves practically the whole population of the United States. Its property sprawls from coast to coast, and its personnel operate in every state and most of the counties of the country. It has the largest amount of assets, the largest number of employees, the largest number of customers, and uses the largest number of banks of any single concern in the country. It is the premier American business, the ace among industrial systems. [Danielian 1939, 26]

In 1924, an AT&T vice president described the Bell System as "really a new sort of thing . . . a publicly owned, privately managed institution." There was no question that AT&T had come a long way in the relatively short period of time since Alexander Graham Bell had obtained the basic patent on his invention of the "talking machine" in 1876.

But AT&T's growth had not been without controversy. Around the turn of the century, following the expiration of Bell's patents, the telephone industry entered a period of unrestrained competition. As a result, AT&T began to lose ground to the independent telephone companies. By 1907, the Bell System had 3,132,000 telephones in service compared to about 2,987,000 for the independents.

Under the guiding hand of J.P. Morgan and other Wall Street financial interests, Theodore Vail took over as president of AT&T and embarked on a plan to rebuild Bell's dominant position. His immediate targets were the telegraph companies and the independent telephone companies. By 1909, AT&T had gained working control of Western Union, and Vail became its president.

Acquisition of independent telephone companies involved both AT&T directly and Morgan & Company acting on AT&T's behalf. Where independent companies held out, they often found themselves isolated, without connection to the facilities of surrounding companies.

Vail set out AT&T's strategy in the 1910 annual report. He called for a telephone system that was "universal, interdependent and intercommunicating, affording opportunity for any subscriber of any exchange to communicate with any other subscriber of any other exchange. . . ." He envisioned a telephone system "as universal and extensive as the highway system of the country which extends from every man's door to every other man's door."

Vail also made it clear that the country would have to pay a price for such a system. He wrote that he did not believe that universal service could be "accomplished by separately controlled or distinct systems nor that there can be competition in the accepted sense of competition." Instead of competition—or its antithesis, a government-owned monopoly—Vail called for a private monopoly subject to regulation. He told AT&T shareholders that Bell's acquisition of competing independents would continue.

However, a number of independents fought back using state antitrust laws. Several companies began to press for federal prosecution under the Sherman Act. The Attorney General intervened to block temporarily a consolidation of independent companies in Ohio which Morgan had purchased.

The Interstate Commerce Commission, which had assumed jurisdiction over limited aspects of interstate telephony in 1910, opened an investigation into AT&T's attempts to monopolize the communications market. These actions brought Bell to the negotiating table.

The result was the Kingsbury Commitment in 1913 under which AT&T promised the government that it would dispose of its stock in Western Union, allow interconnection with its toll facilities for all independents, and refrain from acquiring any directly competing independent telephone companies. The commitment was made in the form of a letter rather than as part of an actual consent decree.

Vail recognized that a new strategy was required to maintain the strength of the Bell System. He renewed his call for universal service and for government regulation as a way to curb wasteful competition. Vail's strategy was to have Bell withdraw from some markets and the independents from others, thereby eliminating the remaining direct or head-to-head competition.

The independents also saw the virtues in détente with AT&T and the advantages of regulation as a way to stabilize the industry. The Vail strategy permitted the growth of a number of large independent telephone companies.

The consolidation that occurred was endorsed, and even encouraged, by the state regulators. Vail's goal of a single unified telephone system was also advanced by President Wilson's decision in 1918 to take control of the telephone and telegraph system as a wartime measure. The telephone system was run by the Postmaster General for a year, and its return to private hands was accompanied by legislation which gave the Interstate Commerce Commission expanded regulatory authority.

Following this brief period of government control, new questions were raised about AT&T's 1913 pledge not to purchase competing telephone companies. Although the Attorney General had rendered an opinion that neither the Kingsbury Commitment nor the antitrust laws themselves precluded consolidation of two local companies into a single system, doubts still persisted as to AT&T's vulnerability. Thus, in 1921, Congress passed legislation which authorized the Interstate Commerce Commission to approve the consolidation of telephone company holdings by acquisition. The amendments were intended to immunize such consolidations from attack under the antitrust laws.

Relations between the Bell companies and the independents were further cemented by AT&T's pledge in 1922 to work cooperatively with the independents, thereby allaying growing fears that AT&T would take undue advantage of its "release" from the constraints of the Kingsbury Commitment. It soon became clear that both Bell and the independents could rely on state and federal regulation to assure them a fair rate of return and that the existence of these regulatory schemes created significant barriers to entry by new competitors.

Vail's strategy was successful. By 1934, AT&T had re-established its dominance in the telephone market. It owned four of every five telephones in the United States. Nearly every major city was served by a Bell operating company, and its long-distance network tied together the country's telephone system. As regulation had grown more pervasive, AT&T had recaptured its monopoly status in the telephone industry.

However, regulation was not to be a constant source of comfort for AT&T. In 1934, federal regulation of the telephone and telegraph industry was transferred from the ICC to a new agency, the Federal Communications Commission. A year later, President Roosevelt signed a joint resolution of Congress "authorizing the [FCC] to investigate and report on the American Telephone & Telegraph Co. and all other companies engaged directly or indirectly in telephone communication in interstate commerce, including all companies related to any of these companies through a holding company structure, or otherwise." The resolution was broadly worded and was accompanied with a special appropriation of $750,000.[3]

The investigation gained momentum in 1936 under the direction of Commissioner Paul A. Walker, Chairman of the FCC's Telephone Division. The focus of the investigation was confined largely to AT&T and its subsidiaries. At first, a nervous AT&T welcomed the investigation. Its chairman, Walter S. Gifford, said publicly, "There are no skeletons in our closet."

And, indeed, AT&T did cooperate. Before long the Commission staff was awash in a sea of paper. But as the investigation dragged on, AT&T grew increasingly concerned. Gifford called the investigation one-sided and complained openly that AT&T was not allowed to cross-examine Commission witnesses or to gain access to staff working papers.[4] Walker became an adversary and the investigation turned into the first real government threat to Bell's monopoly position.

On April 1, 1938, Commissioner Walker released a "Proposed Report." The report has been described as a "free-swinging and broad-based attack on AT&T's ways of conducting its business." [Brooks 1976, 198] It dealt with a number of Bell System practices, but focused on the relationships between AT&T and Western Electric, Bell's manufacturing arm. The Walker Report alleged that Western had overcharged for its equipment and had inflated the telephone rate base driving up prices for consumers. Walker urged direct regulation of Western's prices and called for legislation to force AT&T to purchase its equipment through competitive bidding.

The Walker Report also pointed out the "inability of State commissions to regulate adequately Bell Operating Companies" and suggested that government ownership should be considered if regulation failed. The Report sought vast new authority for the FCC to "review, approve, or disapprove all Bell System policies and practices promulgated by the central management group of [AT&T]," to "review, approve, or disapprove all intercompany contracts," and "to limit the scope of Bell System Activities to the communications field." [Walker Report 1938, 698]

The response to the draft report was swift and negative. The other members of the FCC made it clear that the views were those of Commissioner Walker alone. The findings were attacked in nearly every editorial page in the country. The *Wall Street Journal* termed the report a "travesty." The *New York Herald Tribune* referred to the Commission staff as an "army of government snoopers" and to the Commission itself as "a sinful and incompetent organization." While acknowledging that there was room for improvement in the management and operation of the Bell System, *Business Week* called the investigation "unfair" and "one-sided." AT&T filed a massive rebuttal which contained a point-by-point refutation of what Gifford called the "incorrect, incomplete, and . . . unsound recommendations" of an "unfair" investigation.

When the Commission issued its final report in 1939, it backed away from most of the more controversial findings of the Walker draft. It rejected the recommendation for competition in the supply of equipment in favor of regulation, but stopped short of imposing direct regulation on Western Electric. Other than what it termed "minor exceptions," the FCC said that its existing statutory mandate was adequate, but indicated that additional funds would be required for "the inauguration and development of continuous and efficient administrative processes in this highly technical field of government effort." [FCC Final Report 1939, 602] Ironically, one casualty of this controversial period was the Telephone Division which Walker headed. The Division was abolished in 1937.

Despite the softening of the Commission's final stance, it was acknowledged that the investigation had raised serious concerns about the structure of the Bell System. The seeds planted by the Walker Report germinated during the next decade and ultimately grew into the first government antitrust suit against AT&T and its wholly owned subsidiary Western Electric, which was filed on January 14, 1949.[5]

The suit alleged that "the absence of effective competition has tended to defeat effective public regulation of rates charged to subscribers for telephone service, since the higher the price charged by Western Electric for telephone apparatus and equipment, the higher the plant investment on which the operating companies are entitled to earn a reasonable rate of return." The Justice Department asked that Western Electric be split off from AT&T and from Bell Telephone Laboratories. Western would then be broken into three competing manufacturing concerns, all of which would vie for Bell System business. As Attorney General Tom Clark summarized it, "The chief purpose of this action is to restore competition in the manufacture and sale of telephone equipment now produced and sold almost exclusively by Western Electric at noncompetitive prices." [Antitrust Subcommittee 1959, 33]

AT&T denied the allegations and contended that there were significant advantages to an integrated system. AT&T noted that all elements of the Bell System were subject to extensive regulation by both federal and state agencies and that "in no instance has it been found that the public interest would be served by the disruption of the existing organization. . . ." [Antitrust Subcommittee 1959, 34]

Ironically, later that year, Western Electric agreed to a request by the Atomic Energy Commission that it take over the Sandia Laboratory, a research and design facility for atomic weapons in New Mexico. The government was anxious to utilize Western's management capabilities to accelerate production of atomic weapons to meet the Russian challenge. AT&T took the opportunity to remind the government that divestiture would hamper the Bell System's ability to render such service in the future.

AT&T made several efforts to convince the government to suspend all activity in the suit during the Korean conflict. Bell was supported by the Department of Defense which lobbied on its behalf within the Truman Administration.[6] The Justice Department refused to yield to the pressure, and, on his last day in office, the outgoing Attorney General wrote to AT&T's counsel refusing to issue a formal suspension notice.

Shortly after the Eisenhower Administration took office, AT&T's general counsel met with the new Attorney General Herbert Brownell during a judicial conference at White Sulfur Springs, West Virginia. According to the Bell lawyer, Brownell would not agree that the case should be dismissed, but did suggest that a way might be found to settle the suit "with no real injury to [AT&T's] business." [Antitrust Subcommittee 1959, 54] AT&T followed-up on this conversation by renewing its contacts with the Defense Department and by pressing for a settlement that would not require divestiture of Western Electric.

In a series of meetings with Justice Department officials in 1954 and 1955, AT&T argued strenuously against divestiture. Bell also questioned the strength of the government's case, urging that it should not go to trial. AT&T prepared a memorandum in which it indicated a willingness to discuss a series of points, including making available Western's patents to competing firms, but which did not involve any structural changes.

AT&T stressed that the relationship between Western's prices and Bell System rates was subject to review by the FCC and by state agencies which could disallow any costs that were found to be unreasonable or excessive. On November 30, 1955, the FCC wrote to the Justice Department that "we are of the opinion that the powers encompassed within the existing regulatory framework can provide substantial safeguards against possible abuses in fixing the prices of Western for equipment and services supplied to the telephone companies in the Bell system."[7]

By late December the parties had reached agreement on the terms of a settlement over the pointed objections of the Justice Department's trial staff.[8] On January 24, 1956, the federal court in New Jersey accepted the consent decree after a brief hearing. The decree did not call for divestiture of Western Electric or provide for any of the other elements of structural relief which had been sought by the government seven years earlier. Instead, AT&T was enjoined from engaging "in any business other than the furnishing of common carrier communications services;" Western Electric was barred from manufacturing equipment other than that used by the Bell System; and the defendants were required to license Bell patents to any applicant that agreed to pay a reasonable royalty and agreed to make available their patents to Bell.

Viewed from just about any perspective, the 1956 Consent Decree was a major victory for AT&T. The costly litigation was over, and Bell's regulated monopoly appeared to be intact. Despite the fact that Bell's competitors would now have access to key patents, there would not be much demand for their products since Western could be expected to continue to supply most of the Bell System's needs.

What neither AT&T nor the Justice Department could have contemplated at the time was that the communications marketplace was about to enter a period of profound change, change that would bring with it expanded competition and renewed pressure for the restructuring of the Bell System. That change began in another courtroom almost before the ink was dry on the consent decree.

In November 1956, the U.S. Court of Appeals in Washington, D.C. ruled that customers had the right to use telephone equipment obtained from sources other than the telephone company. In reversing an FCC decision to the contrary, the Court found that AT&T had improperly interfered with "the telephone subscriber's right reasonably to use his telephone in ways which are privately beneficial without being publicly detrimental."

The reversal marked a victory in an eight-year struggle by a small company named Hush-A-Phone. The Hush-A-Phone device was a cup-like device which could be attached to a telephone handset to provide privacy and screen out surrounding noise.

While the real impact of this decision was not felt for another decade, Bell's end-to-end monopoly had been successfully challenged for the first time. Competitive forces had been set in motion which would lead to today's deregulated marketplace for all customer premises equipment from telephones to small switchboards and communicating computer terminals. It was a marketplace quite different from the one AT&T had sought to preserve in the 1956 Consent Decree.

While AT&T and its emerging competitors were engaged in a series of regulatory and judicial battles,[9] concerns about the structure of the Bell System were still apparent. In 1968, a Presidential Task Force completed a study of communications policy which touched on many of the issues that had been raised in the 1949 antitrust case.[10] Although written in an even-handed tone, the section of the report dealing with the domestic common carrier industry noted that "some maintain that independent manufacturers are deterred from attempting greater access [to Bell telephone companies] as a consequence of the industry's structure. . . ." The Report said that "[i]n theory, the carrier's control of manufacturing could lead to a variety of undesirable consequences, such as uneconomic pricing, inadequate response to opportunities for innovation, and inefficiency." [President's Task Force on Communications Policy 1968, 39]

While the Report stated that the Task Force had not had time to gather more than "fragmentary evidence," it pointed out that "[d]issolution of the ownership ties between Bell and Western Electric has sometimes been suggested as the best way of obtaining the full benefits of diversity and competition for the industry." [President's Task Force on Communications Policy 1968, 40] The question of consistency with the antitrust laws "must be left to the Justice Department and to the courts."[11] Even these temperate observations prompted a bitter dissent to the Report by two members, one of whom wrote that he was opposed even to "the discussion of the relationship of Western Union [sic] and ATT [sic]."

Beginning in 1968 with its *Carterfone* decision, the FCC moved more aggressively to open the telephone equipment market to competition. Frustrated by AT&T's efforts to protect its market and by delays in FCC proceedings, competing suppliers looked to the antitrust laws for recourse. By early 1974, 35 private antitrust suits were filed against AT&T and its subsidiaries. In 1972, the federal district court in Hawaii ruled against General Telephone (GTE), the largest of the independent telephone companies, in a suit brought by ITT under the Clayton Act. The court ordered GTE to divest itself of its manufacturing subsidiaries.[12]

During this same period, the Commission had authorized the first long-distance competitors. In 1969, the FCC approved a request filed six years earlier by MCI to begin construction of a private line network between St. Louis and Chicago. Despite bitter opposition from AT&T, the Commission subsequently gave MCI the go-ahead to offer service in 1971. MCI later estimated that the legal and regulatory costs involved in entering the long-distance market were five times greater that the costs of constructing their first network. In May 1971, the Commission took the next step and issued a decision which favored increased competition, generally in the provision of private line services by specialized carriers.

A series of disputes arose as these new carriers sought to connect with the local facilities of the Bell Operating Companies. While the FCC ultimately ordered connection, AT&T's new competitors began to turn to the antitrust laws for protection. Pressure began to mount on the Justice Department to intervene.

On November 20, 1974, the Justice Department re-entered the fray by filing a new antitrust suit against AT&T, Western Electric, and Bell Telephone Laboratories, Inc.[13] The new suit was much more comprehensive than the one filed in 1949. The complaint charged the defendants with monopolizing telecommunications services and products, and sought the divestiture of Western Electric, which was to be split into at least two companies, and of "some or all of the Bell Operating Companies."[14] In the words of one observer, "the suit provided for the possibility, at most, of total dismemberment of the Bell System." [Brooks 1976, 315]

Most of the next six years were spent in battles between the parties over jurisdictional issues and in a lengthy discovery process.[15] Slowly, but surely, the massive case against the world's largest company moved closer to trial.

The trial began on January 15, 1981, just days before President Reagan took office. It was recessed immediately following opening statements amid a flurry of speculation that a negotiated settlement was at hand. Meetings were held between AT&T lawyers and the staff of the Carter Justice Department. Rumor had it that Justice was willing to settle for the divestiture of several of the BOCs and for some restrictions on the relationship between the BOCs, Western Electric, and Bell Labs along the lines suggested by legislation which had been considered in Congress during the previous year and by a key FCC decision.[16] Settlement talks broke down, reportedly because incoming Justice Department officials believed that the settlement terms proposed by their predecessors in the Carter Administration did not deal effectively with AT&T structure. On March 4, 1981, the trial resumed.

Despite pressure from the Department of Defense and the Commerce Department to delay the litigation until Congress could enact comprehensive telephone deregulation legislation that would have stopped short of divestiture in dealing with Bell System structure, the Justice Department pressed its case into the summer. Government lawyers presented nearly 100 witnesses and thousands of documents. At the conclusion of the government's case, AT&T moved to dismiss, but Judge Greene denied the motion. Moreover, Greene stated that the government had presented a strong case and that AT&T would have a difficult time overcoming the weight of the evidence in a number of areas. The vehemence with which Judge Greene responded to AT&T's motion may have signaled to the Bell lawyers that the ultimate outcome of the trial was no longer in doubt and that the time had come to accelerate efforts to work out a settlement.

Nevertheless, following this setback, AT&T began its response. Its defense involved approximately 250 witnesses and tens of thousands of pages of documents. In all, the transcript of the trial record in the case would run over 24,000 pages.

On January 8, 1982, less than two weeks before AT&T was scheduled to complete its direct case, the parties announced that a settlement had been reached. The form of the settlement became immediately controversial. The parties had filed simultaneously a "Modification of Final Judgment," changing the terms of the 1956 Consent Decree, with the district court in New Jersey, and a motion to dismiss the pending antitrust suit with the district court in Washington where Judge Greene had been trying the case.

While a district court judge in New Jersey accepted the modified decree, Judge Greene refused to allow the dismissal motion to be filed. Greene was concerned that the terms agreed to by Justice and AT&T were intended to deal primarily with the pending lawsuit and not with the 1956 Decree.[17] Subsequently, the parties agreed to request that jurisdiction over the 1956 Consent Decree be transferred to Greene's court. After assuming jurisdiction, Greene promptly vacated acceptance of the modified decree and began the lengthy process of review of the terms of the settlement required by the Antitrust Procedures and Penalties Act (generally referred to as the Tunney Act).[18]

Initially, both the Justice Department and AT&T took the position that the Tunney Act did not apply because the settlement had come in the form of an agreement to modify the terms of the existing 1956 Consent Decree. They also argued that the case was no longer formally before Judge Greene inasmuch as the parties had agreed to dismiss the pending action. Judge Greene rejected the Justice Department and Bell arguments in strong language, holding that their "reasoning may most charitably be described as disingenuous."

Because both parties subsequently agreed to submit to the jurisdiction of Judge Greene's court, the Judge never had to rule on the "technical applicability" of the Tunney Act. Instead, Judge Greene proceeded, as he described it, "under the Court's general equitable powers" to apply the Tunney Act procedures. While he may not have established a binding legal precedent, Judge Greene clearly broke new ground in successfully extending the power and prestige of the court.

Despite the initial controversy over form and procedure, it is the substance of the new decree that warrants the attention of this book. The restructuring of AT&T agreed to in the decree will result in a fundamental change in the telecommunications system in this country.

The theory of the new consent decree is quite simple. It is intended to separate the competitive aspects of AT&T's business from the remaining elements of the Bell monopoly. Under terms of the divestiture, AT&T retains its long-distance business (the Long Lines Department), its equipment manufacturing capability (Western Electric), and its research arm (Bell

Labs). AT&T surrenders its 22 local operating companies which have been reorganized into seven regional companies.

The divested local operating companies are required to provide service and access to their "bottleneck" facilities to all long-distance carriers which is "equal in type, quality, and price" to that provided to AT&T. In addition, the Bell Operating Companies are prevented from engaging in any "non-monopoly" business in an effort to eliminate their ability to abuse their position of dominance. The settlement negotiated by the parties specifically barred the divested telephone companies from manufacturing or marketing customer premises equipment, from providing long-distance service, from providing directory advertising such as the *Yellow Pages*, and from offering services where they controlled the information content.

Following the extensive written submissions and oral arguments established under the Tunney Act, Judge Greene convinced the parties to modify a number of these provisions. Most importantly, he forced several changes in the restrictions placed on the BOCs. Judge Greene took these steps out of a concern that the viability of the Bell Operating Companies was threatened by the prohibitions in the original settlement.

As a result of Judge Greene's intervention, the local telephone companies retained their control of directory advertising, including the lucrative *Yellow Pages* which produce an estimated $3 billion in revenue annually. In addition, the local companies are permitted to market telephone equipment as long as it is manufactured by some other entity. Judge Greene also barred AT&T from using the Bell name or logo except in connection with Bell Labs, leaving that trademark in the hands of the divested local operating companies.[19]

At the same time, Judge Greene placed some new restrictions on AT&T. He barred the company from engaging in "electronic publishing" over its own transmission facilities, and he limited the share of the total Bell System debt that would have to be shouldered by each of the divested local companies. Judge Greene also forced the parties to redraw the boundaries of some of the territories within which the Bell Operating Companies are permitted to offer services (the so-called "LATAs" or "Local Access and Transport Areas").

The changes brought about by the settlement of the government's antitrust suit against AT&T alters drastically the telecommunications industry in the United States. In combination with FCC decisions establishing customer charges for access to long-distance networks and requiring the deregulation of telephone equipment, the new AT&T decree is changing the way in which telephone service is provided and paid for in the United States.

The transition from a long period of regulated monopoly and limited competition where one firm dominated all aspects of the telephone business to an environment marked by open entry, rapid technological change and a proliferation of new entrants has been accelerated. In a real sense, this book explores that transition and its impact on the economy, technology, the consumer, federal and state regulation, and society in general.

NOTES

1. Vail was to resign in 1887 after being passed over for president of the parent company. His return to AT&T 20 years later marked one of the most successful periods in the company's history.

2. At the time of its acquisition by Bell, the Western Electric Manufacturing Company had substantial experience in the manufacturing of telephones and telephone equipment which it had gained largely through supplying Western Union during that company's brief foray into the telephone service business.

3. Two more appropriations were made in 1936 and 1937 totaling an additional $750,000. These were quite significant sums at a time when the entire FCC budget was only about $1.5 million.

4. The company conveyed its concern to the public in its annual reports for 1936, 1937, and 1938 in which it took exception to the unfair methods of conducting the investigation. [Page 1941, 173]

5. Brooks suggests a direct connection between the FCC investigation and the 1949 lawsuit: "Holmes Baldridge, an astute Oklahoma lawyer who had served as Commissioner Walker's principal attorney in that investigation, had gone on to join the Justice Department's antitrust division as chief of its general litigation section. In that job he had continued to maintain the position, held by Walker and a minority of his colleagues in 1939, that the public would be better served if AT&T and Western Electric were legally split apart." [Brooks 1976, 234]

6. In addition to the Sandia project, Western Electric was the prime contractor for the Nike Ajax anti-aircraft missile and for several other advanced nuclear weapons systems. Western and Bell Labs also worked extensively on developing the Distant Early Warning air-defense radar system. Brooks notes that "AT&T's sales to the government on defense projects set new peacetime records almost every year in the middle and late 1950s." [Brooks 1976, 253] AT&T began to reduce its work for the government on weapons systems in the aftermath of controversy over the antiballistic missile (ABM) during the period of public disenchantment with the Vietnam War in the late 1960s and early 1970s. As a result, when AT&T attempted to play its Defense Department "card" to derail the subsequent government antitrust suit, it met with less success.

7. The Antitrust Subcommittee noted that the original draft of the Commission's letter, prepared by the staff, was much more guarded and indicated concern about lack of funding needed to exercise its powers. The Subcommittee suggested that extensive lobbying of the Commissioners by AT&T had produced the desired result. [Brooks 1976, 75]

8. One key member of the trial staff refused to sign the agreement because, as he later told the House Subcommittee, "I did not think that this decree could possibly be consistent with the Sherman Act." [Brooks 1976, 84]

9. The history of these struggles is discussed at length in Chapter 3.

10. The Final Report of the President's Task Force on Communications Policy was transmitted to President Johnson in December 1968, but was not released until the following year after demands by the Subcommittee on Communications of the U.S. House of Representatives.

11. The Report unequivocally recommended "access by outside suppliers to the widest extent feasible," reiterating the policy advanced by Commissioner Walker 30 years earlier.

12. Following appeals and further litigation, the parties settled this suit. General Telephone (GTE) was permitted to retain its manufacturing subsidiaries in exchange for an agreement to purchase from outside suppliers and to deal with its own subsidiaries on an "arms-length basis." [*See* discussion in Brock 1981, 295–296.]

13. It is perhaps more than coincidence that one of the primary economic consultants to the Justice Department in this case was Roger Noll, who had served as liaison to the Presidential Task Force for the Council of Economic Advisers. Walter Hinchman, who had served as a Task Force staff member, had become chief of the FCC's Common Carrier Bureau and a major architect of the Commission's pro-competitive policies. Ironically, one of the outside consultants to the Task Force was William Baxter, who, eight years later, was the Assistant Attorney General who negotiated the breakup of the Bell System.

14. The relief sought by the government was modified several times during the pendency of the antitrust suit. At one time, the Justice Department requested divestiture of portions of Bell Labs. However, divestiture of all or some of the BOCs was always one of the primary relief requests. The changes in the relief sought was due, in part, to changes in the marketplace during the course of the litigation. In 1974, AT&T's dominance in the customer premises equipment market was largely unchallenged. By 1982, Western was losing market share rapidly, especially in sales of new PBXs.

15. A key development during this period was the transfer of the case to District Court Judge Harold Greene due to the illness of Judge Waddy (who died in June 1976). Judge Greene moved swiftly and decisively to coordinate discovery and to define the issues. Greene also initiated a process to force the parties to stipulate all uncontested facts and contentions, narrowing the case to 82 segments or episodes. These disputed episodes were further reduced by agreement of the parties prior to trial.

16. In 1980, the House of Representatives had been the focal point for legislation, H.R. 6121, that would have required AT&T to establish a separate subsidiary for competitive services and products with an "arms-length" relationship to other parts of the Bell System. H.R. 6121 was approved by the House Commerce Committee by an overwhelming vote of 34–7 but was prevented from coming before the House of Representatives by the intervention of the House Judiciary Committee whose leadership was concerned that passage of the bill might affect the pending government and private antitrust suits. Early in 1981, the Senate approved S.898, which embodied most of the House language by a margin of 90–2. The FCC adopted an approach which was nearly identical to the House bill in its final decision in the *Second Computer Inquiry*. The Commission ordered AT&T to set up a separate subsidiary in order to offer "enhanced services" and all customer premises equipment. That subsidiary is AT&T Information Systems, which came into being on January 1, 1984.

17. The modified decree did remove the restrictions on AT&T's entry into unregulated markets and on its use of patents that were contained in the 1956 Consent Decree.

18. Judge Greene's use of the Tunney Act procedures is one of the interesting sidebars of the Bell divestiture. Enacted by Congress in 1974, the Tunney Act was designed to permit court review of the terms of consent decrees agreed to by the parties involved in an antitrust action. Before entering the final judgment, the court is required to determine that the settlement decree is in the public interest. The court has the authority to permit outside parties to comment on terms of a settlement and to otherwise satisfy the Act's standard for review.

19. A number of the new regional Bell operating companies have incorporated "Bell" into their new identity, while others have chosen to break with tradition. The announced names for the regional companies are: Pacific Telesis (California and Nevada), U.S. West (far Southwest, Pacific Northwest, and Northern Plains), Southwestern Bell Corporation (Texas and lower Midwest), Ameritech (upper Midwest), Nynex (New York and New England), Bell Atlantic (Middle Atlantic), and BellSouth (Southeast).

3
THE END OF MONOPOLY

Regulatory Change and
the Promotion of Competition

by Richard E. Wiley[1]

The preservation of competition in our economic system generally is closely associated with vigorous enforcement of our nation's antitrust laws. In that regard, the settlement of *United States v. American Telephone and Telegraph Company*, breaking-up AT&T's national monopoly, will be judged by many as a major achievement.

However, the role played by the Federal Communications Commission in promoting a competitive telecommunications industry structure during the preceding 15 years also deserves recognition. In fact, the manner in which AT&T chose to respond to the FCC's pro-competitive decisions in both the terminal equipment and long-distance transmission markets led, in large part, to the AT&T divestiture.

While regulation has been widely criticized in recent times, the FCC's restructuring of the telecommunications industry has benefited the public immeasurably. What was unique about the FCC's efforts was that it used regulation as a tool to accommodate and foster a competitive industry structure.

During the late 1960s and early 1970s, advancements in technology and consumer demand for new services and products proved to be more than a single company could handle. Accordingly, the FCC adopted policies designed to encourage entry into selected markets without jeopardizing a public telephone system that had become the envy of the world.

This chapter reviews the ways in which the FCC brought competition to a highly concentrated industry, and how the competitive market structure that resulted is now paving the way for deregulation in many segments of the telecommunications field.

BACKGROUND: FCC REGULATION PRIOR TO 1968

Regulated Monopoly Era

When the Communications Act of 1934 was enacted, it was widely believed that telephone service was a "natural monopoly." This view was premised on the physical limitations of telephony at that time. Even though numerous telephone and telegraph carriers originally entered the field, it quickly became apparent that duplicative wires, terminal instruments, rights of way, and buildings—either between cities or within cities—made competition impractical. This waste of resources and capital was called "destructive competition."

As a result, a public consensus emerged stating that no geographic location should be served by more than one telephone company. AT&T and its local Bell System Operating Companies became the sole supplier of local telephone services to over 80 percent of the nation's population. The remainder of the country was served by local monopoly independent companies. These local companies all interconnected with AT&T's intercity network for long-distance service. For similar reasons, Western Union monopolized the telegraph industry, the only other electronic telecommunications service of the era.

Of course, the ability of these monopolistic entities to engage in anticompetitive activities was well understood at the time. For precisely this reason, Congress created the FCC in 1934, authorizing it to regulate the telephone and telegraph industries. Among other things, the Communications Act of 1934 directs the FCC to ensure that communications carriers do not overcharge or discriminate.[2]

In addition, Congress sought to use regulation to achieve specific social goals. The Act encouraged the development of universal telephone service and mandated policies to encourage the construction of the most modern, rapid, and efficient telecommunications system possible.[3] These goals were to be pursued, however, in the context of private ownership of telecommunications companies. Congress preferred economic regulation of private business over government ownership and operation of the nation's telecommunications system, a course chosen by nearly every other nation in the world.

Under this scheme, the FCC regulated AT&T and Western Union as essentially private monopolies for the next three decades.[4] The type of regulation during that period, however, was neither formal nor exacting. For the most part, the FCC followed a concept known as "continuing surveillance." If the agency believed AT&T's overall rate of return was too high, for instance, it would simply negotiate a rate reduction with the carrier. The FCC rarely concerned itself with cost-of-service studies or rate structure issues. Similar informal measures would be taken in response to claims of questionable carrier practices.

Technical Developments Undermining the Monopoly Market

Until the mid-1960s, this regulated monopoly market structure worked well. The national policy objectives of affordable, universal telephone service and the construction of the most rapid and efficient system possible were essentially fulfilled.

In the 1950s, however, technological advances began to eliminate many of the "natural monopoly" elements of telecommunications service. Of primary significance was the new microwave technology which overcame the alleged natural monopoly traits of cable-based intercity telecommunications transmission. Second, with the widespread development and application of computers, user needs for high-speed digital communications became increasingly important.

Microwave

Prior to World War II, intercity transmission services were viewed as natural monopolies. Cables connecting telephone and telegraph offices crisscrossed the landscape. During the war, however, the Army Signal Corps developed a new technique for transmitting voice communications by means of radio waves only a few centimeters long (i.e., microwaves). Construction of a microwave voice communications system was faster, more economic, and easier than laying cables. Microwave antenna towers could be placed as much as 35 miles apart, with no need for acquiring any rights-of-way in between.

The subsequent application of this technology to the nation's telephone system was a means of overcoming the natural monopoly characteristics of intercity transmission services.

Computers

The invention of the computer also brought with it a need for new communications services and equipment that had not traditionally been offered by the monopoly telephone and telegraph companies. At first, computers were extremely large in size, housed in special facilities often requiring a user's physical presence. Due to the obvious inefficiencies of that arrangement, the ability to access centrally located computers from remote user terminals became critical. Additionally, as more and more computing devices came into use, the need for computers at different geographic locations to "talk" to each other developed. These physical barriers were ultimately overcome by employing telephone lines to link computers and users to one another.

Expanding computer reliance on telephone company lines soon created another problem. The basic telephone network was originally designed and constructed to carry only human voices. To do that, system designers used "analog" transmission techniques. However, for users to be able to communicate with a central computer, or for computers to talk with each other, an entirely different transmission mode was necessary. Specifically, computers require transmission lines which can accommodate "digital" information. Thus, terminal devices and a network optimized for human voice communications had serious limitations for computer data transmission—limitations which led to significant economic and technological pressures to develop alternative transmission techniques.

But if the computer revolution created a demand for specialized communications services and equipment, it also produced many of the solutions. By the mid-1960s, computer technology was being applied to improve the basic operations of the telephone system. Computers started to replace the electromechanical hardware used to switch telephone messages. Computers also permitted telephone companies to introduce new communications services, such as remote call forwarding, message storage, speed dialing, and so on.

In the process of developing these telecommunications applications for computers, large numbers of firms outside the traditional telephone and telegraph industry acquired technical expertise that was directly transferable to communications. Telecommunications companies were also developing computer processing expertise.

Furthermore, the marriage of computer and communications technologies effectively destroyed the homogeneity of the terminal market. The simple telephone handset could no longer satisfy all of the demands placed on the public telephone network. As a result, serious questions arose as to whether it was in the public interest to rely on a single terminal equipment supplier or whether reliance on a competitive marketplace might be more appropriate.

The FCC recognized the importance of these issues and, in 1965, instituted a proceeding which is commonly referred to as the *First Computer Inquiry*.[5] Primarily as a result of its findings in the *First Computer Inquiry*,[6] the FCC began reassessing the monopolistic market structure it had helped foster. The radically new public needs spawned by the development of data communications altered the way in which the objectives set by Congress in 1934 could best be achieved. While dramatic changes were soon to occur in the terminal equipment and transmission fields, the introduction of competition in each developed separately.

THE EVOLUTION OF CUSTOMER PREMISES EQUIPMENT COMPETITION

Creation of the "Consumers' Right" to Use Their Own Terminals

As communications needs emerged which the Bell System could not meet, AT&T nevertheless prohibited its customers from connecting any device to its lines—no matter how innocuous—if it was not furnished by the telephone company. In one instance, AT&T attempted to enforce this restriction against customers who utilized the Hush-A-Phone, a cup-like device which was placed on the telephone handset to funnel the speaker's voice into the telephone instrument. The device was intended to facilitate private telephone conversations in noisy locations.

When the FCC refused to order the Bell System to remove this limitation, Hush-A-Phone asked the United States Court of Appeals to overturn the Commission's ruling. The Court agreed and held that AT&T had acted unlawfully in disallowing the attachment of the Hush-A-Phone.

In so doing, the Court first enunciated the principle that telecommunications subscribers have a right to use the telecommunications system "in ways which are privately beneficial without being publicly detrimental," and that telephone company regulations which interfere with that right are unreasonable as a matter of law.[7]

After the *Hush-A-Phone* decision, AT&T made some changes in its regulations, but essentially took the position that the *Hush-A-Phone* ruling was limited to its facts. Thus, the general prohibition against connecting independently manufactured terminal equipment, or "customer premises equipment" (CPE), to telephone company lines persisted.

But along came Thomas Carter, an entrepreneur who began marketing to private individuals a device called the "Carterfone." This device acoustically and inductively interconnected mobile radio systems with the wireline telephone system. When the telephone companies refused to allow the device to be used, Carter asked the FCC for relief. Thus, the issue of terminal equipment interconnection was presented to the FCC concurrently with its *Computer I* inquiry.

In March 1968, the FCC concluded that AT&T's tariff prohibiting use of the Carterfone was unreasonable and unlawful. The *Carterfone* case[8] therefore firmly established the consumer's right to connect non-carrier provided, technically compatible equipment to the public telephone network.

As part of the *Carterfone* decision, the Commission also ordered the carriers to submit regulations to protect the telephone system against *technically* harmful devices, but to otherwise allow the customer to provide his own terminal equipment.[9] Subsequently, AT&T filed tariffs which generally allowed free acoustic and inductive interconnection of CPE and communications systems, but which permitted the direct electrical connection of such equipment only through "protective connecting arrangements" (PCAs). Bell maintained that PCAs were required to guard the network against technical harm.

The PCAs could only be acquired from the telephone company, for an extra monthly charge. Moreover, the tariff requirement that PCAs be used in connection with independently manufactured (non-Bell) CPE obviously made such equipment less attractive to users.

In response to claims by independent manufacturers that such devices were therefore anticompetitive, AT&T maintained that they were necessary to preserve the integrity and usefulness of the network. Nevertheless, the FCC initiated informal proceedings to explore the technical feasibility of liberalizing these restrictions.

The FCC Registration Program: Creation of the "Manufacturers Right" to Access Directly the Telephone Network

The FCC's investigation concluded that uncontrolled interconnection of customer-provided facilities to the nationwide telephone system could harm the network. But, it was technically feasible to ease the interconnection provisions of the tariffs without causing any harm through an FCC-administered program to certify compatibility of independently manufactured equipment with the telephone networks.

As a consequence, in 1975, the Commission found the tariff regulations requiring the use of telephone company-supplied connecting arrangements to be unjust and unreasonable. It adopted instead a program of standards and procedures to govern FCC registration of protective circuitry and customer premises equipment to provide the necessary minimal protection against technical harm to the network.[10]

In just a few short years, this FCC registration program spawned a whole new "interconnect" equipment industry. The industry grew rapidly and is today highly competitive—both with AT&T and among its members. In 1982, interconnect companies produced $1.7 billion in revenues and captured significant shares of various terminal equipment markets. In the business office switchboard (or "PBX") market, for example, the interconnect companies accounted for 21 percent of the market in 1982, a figure expected to increase to 31 percent by 1986. Interconnect industry revenues also are expected to triple by 1986.

It thus would appear that the FCC's policies have benefited American consumers by permitting the CPE market to evolve naturally into a multiple supplier market where competitors must utilize state-of-the-art technology and innovative features to capture a portion of the market.

The FCC's *Computer II* Decision: Deregulation of the Competitive CPE Market

Having opened the CPE market to competition, the next major issue confronting the FCC was to decide whether rate (or "tariff") regulation of common carrier-provided CPE was still necessary. With competition alive and well in the CPE market, many wondered whether there was still a need to continue to regulate rates in this area.

They pointed out that rate regulation of some participants in a single market, and not others, tends to skew the natural operations of the marketplace. Interconnect companies could sell or lease terminal equipment free of regulation, whereas common carriers that offered the same equipment had to file tariffs and obtain regulatory approvals. Further, by "bundling" transmission and terminal equipment charges into a single end-to-end rate for interstate service, the FCC was concerned that common carriers might cross-subsidize their competitive equipment offerings by unfairly shifting costs to their monopoly service ratepayers.

In its *Computer II* decision, the Commission addressed these issues, determining that the provision of *all* customer premises equipment—whether by common carriers or not—should be completely free from regulation.[11] As of January 1, 1983, telephone companies have been prohibited from offering new CPE under tariff, and all existing on-premises CPE are being phased out of the regulatory process. To ensure nationwide uniformity in CPE detariffing, the FCC has also preempted the states' authority to regulate CPE rates.

Finally, so that telephone companies do not unfairly burden those who buy unregulated communications services with costs properly attributable to unregulated equipment offerings, the *Computer II* decision adopted certain accounting and/or structural separation requirements. All carriers, except AT&T, must segregate their regulated and unregulated activities by maintaining separate books of account which the FCC can audit to determine whether improper cross-subsidization is occurring. More stringent separation requirements were imposed on AT&T because of its still dominant nationwide position in the CPE market.

Specifically, the Commission required AT&T to form a wholly separate corporate subsidiary to offer unregulated services and equipment. The FCC believes that this "maximum separation" requirement will make it easier to detect the flow of any cross-subsidies and to take quick remedial action to protect AT&T's regulated communications service ratepayers. To conform with this requirement, AT&T Information Systems, Inc., was created. Whether the FCC will extend the separate corporate subsidiary requirement to the divested Bell Operating Companies in 1984 has yet to be decided.[12]

While the *Computer II* decision is extremely important for what it did—forcing all common carriers to detariff and deregulate their provision of CPE—the way it reached that result is equally important. Ever since 1934, the Communications Act has been construed as a mandate from Congress to regulate interstate common carrier activities, and not to allow carriers to deal with the public on an unregulated basis. If circumstances changed, it was thought that only Congress, not the FCC, could alter this fundamental national policy. This traditional view was shattered by the *Computer II* decision.

Through a creative interpretation of the Act, which has been sustained by the federal courts, the FCC decided in *Computer II* that it has the discretion to *forbear* from regulating some common carrier activities, and even to affirmatively require deregulation under certain conditions. In CPE, the Commission first found that nothing in the Communications Act states that common carriers must offer CPE as part of their communications services. The sale of such equipment is completely severable from the offering of communications transmission services. In fact, the FCC observed that the manufacture, distribution, sale, or lease of CPE by non-carriers (such as by independent interconnect companies) has never been rate regulated under the Act.

Second, the agency was quick to point out that, although the provision of CPE in isolation does not constitute a regulated common carrier activity, all CPE is nevertheless within the overall "subject matter" or ancillary jurisdiction of the Commission. The FCC said that CPE falls within the Act's definition of "wire and radio communications" because it is an instrumentality incidental to communications transmission. Accordingly, the Commission asserted its jurisdiction over any kind of terminal equipment connected to a telephone line.

Having established this jurisdictional basis, the FCC then decided to unbundle and detariff common carrier-provided CPE costs from transmission service rates. Observing that the market for CPE had become competitive, the Commission concluded that there was no longer any public interest need to rate regulate common carrier-provided CPE. Market forces would keep CPE prices at reasonable levels.

In addition, by requiring the removal of CPE from transmission charges, the FCC stated that it could better assure cost-based rates for regulated carrier transmission services. Finally, the agency stressed that its requirement for a separate CPE subsidiary for AT&T, and accounting separation for other carriers, was simply a different means (as opposed to tariffs) for fulfilling its obligations under the Act.

The *Computer II* scheme is now well under way. CPE is quickly becoming just another consumer product marketed by specialty phone stores, interconnect companies, department stores, mail-order outlets and, of course, telephone companies and other carriers. A wide variety of styles, quality, and prices are available. Within ten years, the whole idea of federal regulation of CPE probably will be foreign to the public. Yet, only through the active regulatory efforts of the FCC could these achievements have occurred when they did.

THE EVOLUTION OF INTERCITY TRANSMISSION SERVICE COMPETITION

Benefits similar to those which have come to pass in the CPE field have come from competition in intercity transmission services. As discussed above, prior to the 1960s, transmission services were viewed as natural monopolies. Only AT&T and Western Union publicly offered intercity services, and those services generally were limited to basic voice and record transmission. The emergence and proliferation of computers, however, created a demand for specialized dedicated or "private line" circuits which were not provided by AT&T or Western Union. And, as indicated, microwave radio provided a technological means of overcoming the "natural monopoly" characteristics of intercity private line transmission.

Above 890: A Crack in the Wall

In the 1950s, when the three newly established American television networks needed to transmit television signals to their affiliated stations across the country, AT&T provided transmission facilities primarily with coaxial cable. But, when the networks began to seriously consider the establishment of their own private microwave network, AT&T switched to microwave for its television signal relay services despite its initial investment in cable. It did so because privately-owned microwave transmission networks proved to be a competitive threat to its leased coaxial cable service.

The option of constructing a private microwave network was created by the FCC in a 1959 order known as the *Above 890* decision.[13] The Commission found in *Above 890* that an adequate number of microwave frequencies were available to fulfill the reasonably foreseeable needs of both common carrier *and* private microwave systems. As a result, AT&T was impelled by competition with private microwave networks to hasten its development of microwave technology for its own network.

Not only did the *Above 890* decision cause AT&T to convert to more efficient transmission facilities, but it also brought about *price* competition. Fearing the loss of business that could occur if its largest customers decided to construct their own private communications networks, AT&T filed its first "Telpak" tariff in 1961. Telpak consisted of bulk quantities of private line circuits offered at substantial "volume discounts" from the rates for individual private line circuits.

Questions were immediately raised as to whether Telpak rates were unduly discriminatory or otherwise below cost. After years of hearings, the FCC concluded that some Telpak rates were justified to meet the competitive threat posed by private microwave (i.e., the "competitive necessity" doctrine), but that other Telpak rates had not been shown by AT&T to be fully compensatory.[14] Because the Commission's "continuing surveillance" approach to regulation had never required AT&T to identify the costs associated with each of its individual interstate services, a determination about the overall lawfulness of Telpak was put aside pending the outcome of another Commission proceeding (Docket 18128) to investigate AT&T's cost allocation practices.

Specialized Common Carriers: The True Beginning

Although the *Above 890* decision brought a kind of competition to telecommunications transmission services, only a handful of very large organizations possessed both the need and the financial resources to install a private microwave service *for hire* that really gave momentum to the move toward competition. But, in 1969, a new company known as Microwave Communications, Inc. (MCI) filed an application with the FCC for authority to construct a limited common carrier microwave system to provide specialized voice and data services between Chicago and St. Louis. MCI's proposed services were confined to transmissions between MCI's microwave sites, thereby making it necessary for each subscriber to obtain his own communications link (or "local loop") from his premises to MCI's offices. MCI's proposed rates were lower than those offered by AT&T or Western Union for comparable private line services.[15]

AT&T and Western Union strongly objected to MCI's application. Chief among their objections was that MCI planned to "cream skim"—that is, operate only high-density routes where lower fixed costs per channel permit lower rates with higher profits. They argued that MCI's tactics were not in the public interest because the established carriers were required by the Commission to serve all geographic areas. Thus, to compete with MCI, the carriers maintained that they would be forced to discontinue the practice of averaging the costs of high and low density routes to arrive at a uniform nationwide average rate structure. Without nationwide averaging, private line rates would increase except between major cities.

By a 4–3 vote, the Commission found that competition in the common carrier field, like that proposed by MCI, was in the public interest and granted its application.[16] The FCC rejected the argument that the new carrier would be cream skimming. It said that MCI proposed to offer "new and different" services not then provided by the established interstate carriers.[17]

Shortly after the *MCI* decision, the Commission was inundated with hundreds of applications by other entities desirous of constructing microwave facilities to provide specialized common carrier services in various parts of the country. The applications contained a wide variety of public offerings, including a nationwide switched digital network specifically engineered for computer data transmissions.

Out of concern that the growing demand for data communications would not be met and that other new and innovative services might not develop, the FCC decided that these myriad applications could be more effectively handled through the development of an overall policy, rather than reviewing each application individually. It therefore initiated a rulemaking which culminated in the *Specialized Common Carrier* decision.[18]

The *Specialized Common Carrier* decision was significant in that it established a general policy in favor of new entries in the private line and specialized common carrier markets. The Commission noted that these markets, particularly for data communications, were growing rapidly and were expected to continue to rapidly expand.

The specialized common carrier applicants, rather than entering a fixed market with established services, were seeking to develop new services and markets. Thus, they could be expected to satisfy demands which were not being met by the existing carriers to expand the size of the total communications market. Permitting the entry of specialized common carriers would provide data users with the flexibility and wider range of choices they required. Moreover, competition in the private line market was expected to stimulate technical innovation and the provision of those types of communications services which would attract and hold customers.

Because the specialized carriers would be in direct competition with AT&T in the private line market, the FCC acknowledged that "departure from uniform nationwide pricing practices may be in order and in such circumstances will not be opposed by the Commission."[19]

AT&T subsequently filed its "Hi-Lo" tariff which sought to depart from nationwide average pricing for individual private line circuits. Although the Hi-Lo rates went into effect in June 1974, the FCC concluded after a hearing that AT&T failed to cost justify those rates and declared the Hi-Lo tariff to be null and void.[20]

In response to the *Hi-Lo* decision, AT&T filed another deaveraged private line tariff in April 1976, known as "Multi-Schedule Private Line" (MPL) service.[21] The FCC allowed the MPL rates to take effect, subject to resolution of another proceeding begun to explore methods of ensuring that AT&T's monopoly ratepayers did not improperly cross-subsidize its competitive services.

The *Specialized Common Carrier* decision also recognized that the new specialized carriers would need to interconnect with local monopoly telephone companies to complete their transmission services. Without guaranteed access to these facilities, the development of full and fair competition in the interstate transmission markets could not occur. Accordingly, the Commission issued a broad directive to telephone companies to make their local facilities available to the new carriers, on a reasonable and non-discriminatory basis, for the local origination and termination of their intercity traffic.[22]

Although Bell initially provided dedicated local loops to the specialized common carriers, it refused to provide interconnections for certain private line services which originated or terminated over the local public telephone exchange. Bell argued that the *Specialized Common Carrier* decision did not require such interconnections. The FCC disagreed, ordering the Bell System companies to stop denying specialized carriers reasonable interconnection services similar to those provided by AT&T.[23]

Domestic Satellite Services: "Open Skies"

In 1972, one year after the *Specialized Common Carrier* decision, the FCC adopted a similar competitive entry policy toward domestic satellite communications networks.[24] The Commission said that competitive entry would demonstrate the extent to which satellite technology could provide specialized services more economically and efficiently than terrestrial facilities. The FCC felt that competitive sources of supply for specialized services, both among satellite licensees and between satellite and terrestrial systems, would encourage service and technical innovation, as well as minimal costs to the public.

The Commission recognized that to gain a multiple entry policy, the incentive for competitive entry by financially responsible satellite system entrepreneurs must be meaningful, and not merely token. And, to ensure that real opportunity for entry would not be frustrated by any particular applicant, the Commission imposed certain conditions on AT&T's entry into the domestic satellite market, prohibiting AT&T from utilizing its satellite facilities for competitive private line services for three years.[25]

With approval of the FCC's "open skies" policy, four carriers, RCA, Western Union, Satellite Business Systems, and American Satellite, established domestic satellite transmission systems. Their success spawned new applications. In 1983, the FCC authorized a total of 38 new satellites to be in orbit by 1987.

Also, in 1983, the FCC reduced the spacing between satellites from four degrees to two degrees to permit even greater entry into the satellite transmission services market.[26] In addition, the Commission has authorized the sale of individual satellite transponders on a non-common carrier basis.[27] Satellite capacity is therefore now available not only from regulated domestic satellite carriers, but from private operators as well. Thus, as a result of active FCC regulation, the domestic satellite market, along with the terminal equipment field, has become one of the most dynamic and competitive industries in American business.

"Value-Added" and Resale Carriers

Still another FCC policy of the 1970s—the *Resale and Shared Use* decision—contributed to the development of competition in telecommunications services. "Value-added networks" (VANs) first appeared in 1973 with FCC approval of a packet-switched communications network offered by Packet Communications, Inc.[28] The VANs emerged to serve data communications users requiring different private line services than were available from the existing carriers. VAN carriers simply lease basic private line circuits from other common carriers, attach computers or other devices to those circuits which will perform additional functions (or "added-value"), and then resell the new service to the public.

In authorizing Packet Communications, Inc., the FCC recognized that the entry of "value-added" carriers into the communications services market would affect the structure of the communications industry. Nevertheless, it said that entry should be permitted because it would introduce new and improved means for meeting consumers' data transmission requirements in a manner not available from any other type of carrier. The Commission pointed to its philosophy in the *Specialized Common Carrier* decision, as relevant and supportive of a competitive environment for the development and sales of the type of services proposed.

The authorization of Packet Communications and other VANs was followed in 1976 by a more general FCC policy decision favoring unlimited resale and shared use of private line services and facilities. In its *Resale and Shared Use* decision, the FCC held that any tariffs prohibiting resale and shared use were unjust and unreasonable as a matter of law.[29] However, because resellers (as opposed to sharers) reoffer interstate communications services to the public for hire, the FCC determined that such entities are common carriers and, therefore, should be subject to regulation under the Communications Act.

The impact on the private line market of the *Resale and Shared Use* decision was immediate. AT&T, for example, anticipated that the removal of tariff restrictions on the resale—its bulk discount private line offering—

would cause a substantial loss in company revenues. With resale and sharing, arbitrageurs (both resellers and sharers) could aggregate individual user needs in order to meet the minimum private line circuit subscription requirements necessary to qualify for the lower Telpak rates. Rather than face this possibility, AT&T discontinued its Telpak offering.[30]

The *Execunet* Cases: The Last Barriers Fall

In July 1977, just one year after the Commission adopted an open entry policy for the resale carrier private line market, the United States Court of Appeals for the District of Columbia Circuit issued its landmark *Execunet* decisions.[31] The Court reversed FCC decisions limiting MCI and other specialized carriers to private line services and held that the agency must allow the specialized carriers to offer ordinary long-distance telephone service to the public in competition with AT&T—even though the FCC had never intended to permit such competition in any of its prior rulings. The ramifications of the *Execunet* cases have had a profound and lasting effect on the telecommunications industry and the public.

MCI began to offer its Execunet service in October 1974. A few months after the service was initiated, AT&T complained to the FCC that Execunet was simply regular long-distance message telephone service (MTS)—not a specialized common carrier service. AT&T maintained that MCI was therefore in violation of the *Specialized Common Carrier* decision restricting interstate carrier competition to the dedicated private line and specialized service field. AT&T further alleged that this placed MCI in violation of the service limitations included in its FCC microwave licenses. The FCC agreed with AT&T's position, and ordered MCI to cease and desist from its offering of Execunet.

Judge Skelly Wright reversed the FCC decision, reasoning that the agency had never said that AT&T's monopoly on long-distance public telephone service was in the public interest. Without such a finding, the Court ruled that the FCC erred in restricting the type of services that MCI could offer over its previously authorized microwave facilities.

The next *Execunet* controversy occurred shortly after Wright's decision, when MCI attempted to obtain more interconnections to Bell System's local exchange facilities for its Execunet service. In response to an AT&T petition, the FCC held that MCI was not entitled to additional interconnections for Execunet because the Commission had never conducted a hearing requiring AT&T to connect its local facilities for public switched-message services offered by other interstate carriers. The scope of AT&T's interconnection obligations extended only to interstate specialized and private line services, as established by the *Specialized Common Carrier* decision.

Once again, MCI sought judicial intervention and, as before, Judge Wright held in the *Execunet II* decision that the FCC erred. He concluded that, contrary to the Commission's view, the scope of the interconnection obligation established by the Commission in the *Specialized Common Carrier* decision was broad enough to include services like MCI's Execunet. Moreover, in an *Execunet III* case,[32] Judge Wright extended this interconnection obligation beyond the Bell System Companies to all independent local exchange telephone companies.

After these rulings, the FCC accepted the invitation of the Court in the *Execunet I* case and conducted a hearing into whether competition in the long-distance public telephone market would serve the public interest. In 1980, the Commission formally opened the public-switched telephone service market to competitive entry.[33]

MTS and WATS Resale

By 1980, the FCC had authorized competition in all interstate transmission markets. However, the tariffs of most interstate carriers still contained prohibitions which restricted the resale and shared use of public-switched long-distance services, like MTS and WATS. These tariff restrictions had their origins in pre-*Execunet* times and generally were intended to prevent the aggregation of small MTS users into groups that would resell or share AT&T's lower priced WATS services. Migration of MTS users to WATS, AT&T argued, would necessitate increases in long-distance telephone rates for the average consumer.

As with the resale and shared use of private line services, the FCC found these claims to be unfounded. Consequently, in 1980, it ordered the removal of these tariff restrictions.[34] Today, well over 200 resale carriers offering interstate public-switched message services have been authorized by the FCC.

THE NEED FOR REGULATED COMPETITION: PROBLEMS OF A DOMINANT CARRIER IN COMPETITIVE MARKETS

FCC policy decisions have opened virtually every segment of the telecommunications industry to competitive entry. But changes in policy do not instantly transform an historically monopoly-based industry into a fully competitive one. Even though MCI earned more than $1 billion in revenue in 1982, AT&T still controls over 95 percent of the interstate transmission market. Moreover, interstate access to essential exchange facilities is still controlled by local monopoly telephone companies.

Under these circumstances, the FCC has continued to use its regulatory powers to ensure the transition from a monopoly to a fully competitive marketplace. For the most part, regulation is likely to continue in three areas: 1) AT&T cost allocation, 2) interconnection to local exchange facilities, and 3) access charges.

AT&T Cost Allocation

One of the most vexing problems in establishing competition in intercity services is cross-subsidy. The heart of the cross-subsidy issue is the coexistence of AT&T's participation in monopoly and competitive markets. For years, the FCC has struggled to find a way to permit AT&T to offer competitive services but, at the same time, to keep those operations separated from its regulated monopoly services. The task has not been easy.

Simply put, the FCC's concern has been that if AT&T sets noncompensatory rates for its competitive communications services, the company might subsidize them with revenues collected from monopoly services (residential and commercial long-distance telephone service). Detection and prevention of this kind of harmful cross-subsidy between services is critical to protecting users and to ensuring that AT&T's competitors are not unfairly driven out of the market.

The manner in which communications services should be priced to avoid unlawful cross-subsidies has been the subject of numerous FCC proceedings, most notably in its Docket 18128 proceeding. At that time, only the specialized and private line services markets were open to competition. AT&T maintained that its competitive services should be priced to recover their direct costs, and that all of the company's unattributable joint and common costs (such as overhead) should be borne by the basic monopoly services for which the AT&T network was originally constructed. AT&T contended that the long-run incremental costs (LRIC) of providing its competitive private line services would yield fully compensatory rates.

In its Docket 18128 decision, the Commission rejected LRIC in favor of a fully distributed costing (FDC) methodology for allocating joint and common costs.[35] Under FDC, all of AT&T's services are required to bear a proportionate measure of the company's unattributable costs. The Commission found that the FDC methodology was the best way to ensure that the ratepayers of AT&T's monopoly services were not exploited in the name of competition. The Commission found this to be especially true in the case of AT&T's particular LRIC methodology, because AT&T reserved for itself which of its services would be deemed "incremental" for ratemaking purposes.

On appeal, the Commission's choice of FDC was upheld by the United States Court of Appeals for the District of Columbia Circuit in *Aeronautical Radio, Inc. v. FCC*.[36] Since then, the FCC has prescribed an interim cost allocation manual for use by AT&T in computing its interstate rates.[37] These regulatory measures should provide reasonable assurance that the rates for each of AT&T's major service categories are based on cost.

Interconnection to Local Exchange Facilities

Another area which is critical to the development and maintenance of a fully competitive market structure is equal access for all interstate carriers to local exchange facilities. As mentioned above, the FCC imposed an equal access obligation on local exchange carriers in its *Specialized Common Carrier* decision. Later, it launched enforcement proceedings to ensure that these obligations were met. Nonetheless, the need for continued FCC regulation in this area is just as critical today as it ever was, because equal access is still not available to AT&T's long-distance competitors.

Typically, interstate carriers construct or lease their own intercity networks. But, they must generally utilize the exchange facilities of local monopoly telephone companies to reach the homes and offices of their subscribers. From an interstate carrier's perspective, the local exchange represents a "gateway" or "bottleneck" through which its interstate traffic must pass. In the absence of regulation, the entities which monopolize these essential bottleneck facilities can charge a very high toll, discriminating against, or even refusing access to, others. In the telecommunications industry, this situation has created several obstacles to the achievement of full and fair competition.

To begin with, a serious problem faced by MCI and other new carrier entrants has been that their primary long-distance competitor, AT&T, also owned and controlled virtually all of the exchanges serving the major U.S. cities. This control is essentially the same as if one airline owned most of the major airports and unilaterally decided the manner, time, and price by which its competitors could have access to those facilities.

In such circumstances, the incentive for AT&T to favor its own interstate operations is obvious. AT&T's efforts to impede competition by such means was a primary reason for the divestiture of its local Bell System Operating Companies.[38]

This is not to say, however, that other monopoly local exchange carriers—whether affiliated with an interstate carrier or not—have neither the ability nor the incentive to favor their own interstate affiliates or deny access to others. Thus, when the Lincoln Telephone and Telegraph Company refused to provide MCI with the interconnections necessary to terminate its Execunet services, the FCC prevented that local telephone company from frustrating national policy in favor of competition.[39]

While regulation has been used to secure the right to interconnect, it has also been a means to bring about technical changes. For example, the specialized and resale common carriers (often called "Other Common Carriers" or OCCs) currently receive a form of interconnection inferior to that provided to AT&T. For example, subscribers to an OCC's services must typically own a push-button telephone (OCC interconnections do not recognize dial pulses), push 10 to 11 extra digits to complete a call, use access codes for purposes of billing, and tolerate a lower quality of voice transmission. This puts the OCCs at a significant competitive disadvantage.

The availability of equal access is therefore essential to a truly competitive marketplace. Accordingly, the FCC recently initiated a proceeding designed to achieve technical interconnection parity for the OCCs by the early 1990s, if not sooner.[40] The divested Bell Operating Companies must also provide equal access to all interstate carriers under the terms of the Modified Final Judgment entered in the AT&T antitrust case.

Access Charges

Ensuring interconnection rights and equality of access are not the only areas which may require further FCC regulation. The prices which local exchange carriers charge the OCCs for their interconnections have been, and will continue to be, an especially important factor in a fully competitive telecommunications marketplace.

Immediately after the *Execunet* decision, AT&T filed its first so-called "ENFIA" tariff,[41] raising the interconnection charges for MCI's MTS/WATS-equivalent services by nearly 300 percent. MCI argued that, having lost the battle to keep it out of the ordinary long-distance telephone business, AT&T was now trying to make it too expensive for the OCCs to compete.

In response, AT&T contended that because the interconnection charges it paid to local telephone companies for its MTS and WATS services included a subsidy for local service, fairness required that all carriers offering MTS/WATS-type services compensate local exchange carriers on the same basis.

To resolve this major tariff controversy, extensive negotiations between AT&T and the OCC industry were conducted under the aegis of the FCC. Finally, both sides reached a "rough justice" ENFIA settlement agreement.[42] Under that agreement, the OCCs receive a discount from the interconnection charges paid by AT&T. The discount is primarily designed to reflect the OCCs' inferior interconnection arrangements. As equal access becomes available, the OCC discount is likely to be reduced or eliminated, as appropriate.

ENFIA, however, was intended as a temporary expedient to facilitate the competition mandated by the *Execunet* decisions. In its landmark *Access Charge* proceeding (CC Docket No. 78–72), the FCC devised a long-term solution to access charges, calling for a dramatic change in the way the American public will pay for long-distance telephone service.[43]

When the FCC's new plan takes effect, interstate carriers will no longer be solely responsible for covering the cost of all the local exchange facilities used to originate and terminate interstate calls. This responsibility has been divided between telephone subscribers and interstate carriers. Telephone subscribers will pay directly for the interstate costs associated with the copper wire which runs from homes and offices, over telephone poles or through underground conduits, to the telephone company central office. Interstate carriers will pay for the lines and switches necessary to connect their interstate networks to the local telephone company.

Under the new access scheme, the subscriber access line charge will be a flat monthly fee, to be paid whether or not the subscriber makes any long-distance calls. These charges will be phased in over a 6-year period. The FCC has set the initial monthly fees for interstate access at about $2 per each residential and $6 per each business line. By 1990, the access for every subscriber could climb to as high as $11 per month. Of course, as the costs of these wires are shifted to subscribers, AT&T's long-distance toll charges are expected to decline by approximately 15–30 percent.

In its *Access Charge* decision, the FCC attempted to develop a unified system of cost-based charges to promote competition and preserve universal telephone service. To do that, the FCC essentially decided to redistribute interstate exchange plant costs to the entity which produces those costs, and to require rates consistent with the economic characteristics of the relevant plant (e.g., flat monthly charges for fixed exchange costs and usage charges for variable costs).

Requiring subscribers to pay a mandatory flat monthly fee for interstate access—even though no interstate calls are made—has been severely criticized, sparking the introduction of numerous bills in Congress to repeal the Commission's *Access Charge* decision. On November 10, 1983, the House of Representatives voted overwhelmingly to pass H.R. 4102, which, among other things, prohibits the FCC from imposing residential access charges. In the face of this mounting political pressure, on January 19, 1984, the FCC postponed implementation of its *Access Charge* plan until 1985. At this juncture, the future of the FCC's *Access Charge* plan is uncertain.

DEREGULATION IN EARNEST

Deregulation is the final step in the transformation of the American telecommunications industry. Deregulation has been a cornerstone of recent Administration, Congressional, and FCC policies.

In *Computer II*, the FCC mandated the deregulation of CPE, as discussed above. But it also decided not to regulate 'enhanced" interstate communications services (which it defined to include offerings incorporating some element of computer processing). The enhanced services category encompasses many carriers that heretofore had been regulated, such as the VANS.

Computer II also deregulated many transmission services that incorporate store-and-forward or other computer processing applications. As with CPE, however, the *Computer II* decision permits AT&T to offer such services only through a separate subsidiary.

In keeping with its deregulation trend, the FCC also decided that not all common carriers need be subject to the same degree of economic regulation. For carriers offering basic pipeline transmission services, the FCC devised a scheme of "variable regulation" in its *Competitive Carrier I* proceeding.[44] Under that scheme, the Commission classifies carriers into two categories— dominant or non-dominant—according to their level of market power. AT&T and satellite carriers have been declared to be dominant, whereas MCI, GTE Sprint, and other specialized carriers are treated as non-dominant.

The degree of regulation applied to non-dominant carriers has been significantly reduced as a result of this policy. Among other changes, non-dominant carriers' rates are considered presumptively lawful, certification requirements are reduced, and the public notice and cost support regulations applicable to tariff filings have been streamlined.

The Commission expanded its deregulation of common carriers in the *Competitive Carrier II* decision.[45] In that proceeding, the Commission ruled that it no longer needed to regulate resale carriers of basic terrestrial communications services. Entities that desire to resell AT&T's WATS service to the public, for example, do not even have to apply to the FCC for common carrier operating authority. Nor must they file rates with the Commission for their interstate services. The Commission reasoned that such resale carriers have little opportunity to overcharge or discriminate because the rates of the underlying carrier remain regulated. In addition, the competitive resale market will ensure that transmission charges stay within a reasonable range.

On November 2, 1983, the FCC extended its deregulatory policies even further. In its *Competitive Carrier IV* decision, the Commission decided that even facilities-based non-dominant carriers, such as MCI and GTE Sprint, should be relieved of tariff filing and facilities certification requirements.[46] As a result, AT&T is basically the only interstate common carrier subject to regulation, and the FCC is now considering whether AT&T should be deregulated.[47]

THE ROLE OF CONGRESS

Although Congress approved no major legislation during this period, it has been a significant force in influencing telecommunications policy. Its view also changed substantially during this period.

In 1976, some 200 members of the House cosponsored the Communications Consumer Reform Act. That bill would have ended nearly all competition in telecommunications services. It almost passed, due primarily to telephone company lobbyists who claimed that the new FCC policies were going to cause technical and economic harm to the nation's telephone system, at the expense of consumers.

While the Communications Consumer Reform Act did not pass, it focused Congressional attention on the changes taking place in the telecommunications industry. Since then, subcommittees have thoroughly investigated the field. Several Communications Act "rewrites" were introduced in both houses of Congress, ironically, fostering competition in telecommunications as national policy.

Startled by the near passage of the Communications Consumer Reform Act of 1976, the FCC adopted a methodical and studious approach to the introduction of competition. The Court of Appeals upset that strategy, however, by ruling that the FCC's 1977 *Execunet* decision erred in holding that public long-distance telephone service was closed to entry by would-be competitors.

By 1978, Congressional views had changed drastically. The 1978 *Execunet* rulings did not cause a legislative reversal of the preceding years of pro-competitive FCC decisions, as some feared might happen. With Congress pressing for full competition in all markets at the earliest possible time, the Commission issued a rapid-fire series of rulings incorporating nearly all the substantive aspects of the Congressionally-drafted "rewrites." Those decisions, in combination with divestiture, accomplished most of the goals sought by the legislative proposals.

In 1983, Congressional interest in telecommunications legislation again rose in the wake of the FCC's *Access Charge* decision. Fearing that the combination of the AT&T divestiture, access charges, the deregulation of terminal equipment, and other FCC actions moving to a cost-based environment could threaten universal telephone service, over 16 bills were introduced proposing different ways to ensure the continued availability of affordable basic telephone service within a competitive industry structure.

THE FUTURE

Further common carrier deregulation appears to be the logical next step in the evolving telecommunications policy. Common sense dictates that regulations established to protect the public from the abuses of a monopolist need not be maintained when competition has supplanted monopoly. Thus, as with CPE and terrestrial resale carriers, the areas of domestic satellite communications and specialized data transmission services may no longer require economic regulation by the FCC. Instead, the Commission's role may be to act only when necessary to preserve or foster competition.

AT&T, however, may continue to be subject to FCC oversight (or stringent separation requirements) as it participates in competitive markets and continues to provide monopoly public telephone services. Precisely how much regulation of AT&T is necessary, and what kind, will continue to be the subject of considerable Congressional and FCC debate. Too little regulation could retard the growth of competition, and too much could unfairly hamper AT&T's ability to compete. The resolution of these questions will have an important bearing in determining whether the progress made over the last 15 years will continue.

NOTES

1. Assisting in the preparation of this chapter were Danny E. Adams and Howard D. Polsky. Both were former members of the FCC's Common Carrier Bureau staff.

2. 47 U.S.C. Sections 201(b), 202(a).

3. 47 U.S.C. Section 151.

4. In fact, in 1943, Congress confirmed its earlier policy determination that a regulated monopoly market structure would best serve the nation's needs, enacting Section 222 of the Communications Act which gave the FCC the authority to approve the merger of the Postal Telegraph Company into Western Union (the only two nationwide telegraph carriers) so as to create a legal monopoly, exempt from the antitrust laws, and subject to FCC regulation. *See* Application for Merger of Western union and Postal Telegraph, Inc., 10 F.C.C. 148 (1943). Thirty-six years later, the Commission found that competition was again feasible in the domestic telegraph market and eliminated Western Union's monopoly status. *See* Graphnet Systems, Inc., 71 F.C.C. 2d 471 (1979), *aff'd sub nom.* Western Union Tel. Co. v. FCC, 665 F2d 1112 (D.C. Cir. 1981). Shortly thereafter, Congress ratified the FCC's new policy and amended Section 222 to promote the development of a fully competitive domestic telegraph industry pursuant to the "Record Carrier Competition Act of 1981." P.L. 97–130, 95 Stat. 1687.

5. Notice of Inquiry,*In re* Regulatory and Policy Problems Presented by the Interdependence of Computer and Communication Services and Facilities (Docket No. 16979), 7 F.C.C. 2d 11 (1966), *further notice,* 17 F.C.C. 2d 587 (1969).

6. Computer Use of Communications Facilities (Final Decision), 28 F.C.C. 2d 267 (1971), *aff'd in part sub nom.,* GTE Service Corp. v. FCC, 474 F.2d 724 (2d Cir. 1973).

7. Hush-a-Phone v. United States, 238 F.2d 266 (D.C. Cir. 1956).

8. Carterfone, 13 F.C.C.2d 420, *recon. denied,* 14 F.C.C.2d 571 (1968).

9. AT&T (Foreign Attachments), 15 F.C.C.2d 605, *recon. denied,* 18 F.C.C.2d 871 (1969).

10. Interstate and Foreign Message Toll Telephone (Docket No. 19528) (First Report and Order), 56 F.C.C.2d 593 (1975), *aff'd sub nom.* North Carolina Util. Comm'n v. FCC, 537 F.2d 787 (4th Cir.), *cert. denied* 429 U.S. 1027 (1976); Second Report and Order, 58 F.C.C.2d 739 (1976), *aff'd sub nom.* North Carolina Util. Comm'n v. FCC, 552 F.2d 1036 (4th Cir.), *cert. denied,* 434 U.S. 874 (1977).

11. Second Computer Inquiry, 77 F.C.C.2d 384 (1980), *recon.,* 84 F.C.C.2d 50, *further recon.,* 88 F.C.C.2d 512 (1981), *aff'd sub nom.* Computer and Communications Indust. Ass'n v. FCC, 693 F.2d 19 (D.C. Cir. 1982), *cert. denied,* 51 U.S.L.W. 3824 (May 17, 1983).

12. Notice of Proposed Rulemaking, CC Docket No. 83-115, FCC 83-71 (released March 4, 1983).

13. Allocation of Frequencies in the Bands Above 890 Mc., 27 F.C.C. 359 (1959), *recon.,* 29 F.C.C. 825 (1960).

14. *See* American Trucking Ass'n. v. FCC, 377 F.2d 121 (D.C. Cir. 1966), *cert. denied,* 386 U.S. 943 (1967).

15. MCI claimed that it could offer lower rates because its service utilized smaller channels with less capacity, and customers would be sharing these channels. Moreover, unlike AT&T and Western union, MCI pointed out that it was not offering a "through" or "end-to-end" service, which included the cost of local loops. MCI estimated that its service would attract a maximum of 204 small business subscribers.

16. Microwave Communications, Inc., 18 F.C.C.2d 953 (1969).

17. Ibid., 961.

18. Specialized Common Carrier Services, 29 F.C.C.2d 870 (1971), *aff'd sub nom.* Washington Util. and Transp. Comm'n v. FCC, 513 F.2d 1142 (9th Cir.), *cert. denied,* 423 U.S. 836 (1975).

19. 29 F.C.C.2d, 915.

20. AT&T, 58 F.C.C.2d 362 (1976).

21. AT&T, 74 F.C.C.2d 1 (1979), *recon.,* 85 F.C.C.2d 549 (1981).

22. 29 F.C.C.2d, 940.

23. Bell System Tariff Offerings, 46 F.C.C.2d 413 (1974), *aff'd sub nom.* Bell Tel. Co. of Pennsylvania v. FCC, 503 F.2d 1250 (3rd Cir. 1974), *cert. denied,* 422 U.S. 1026 (1975).

24. Domestic Communications-Satellite Facilities (DOMSAT), First Report and Order, 22 F.C.C.2d 86 (1970); Second Report and Order, 35 F.C.C.2d 844 (1972), *aff'd sub nom.* Network Project v. FCC, 511 F.2d 786 (D.C. Cir. 1975).

25. The moratorium was terminated in 1979. Satellite Private Line Services, 72 F.C.C.2d 895 (1979).

26. Report and Order (CC Docket No. 81-704), FCC 83-184 (released August 16, 1983).

27. Domestic Fixed Satellite Transponder Sales, 90 F.C.C.2d 1238 (1982).

28. Packet Communications, Inc., 43 F.C.C.2d 922 (1973).

29. Resale and Shared Use, 60 F.C.C.2d 261, *recon.*, 62 F.C.C.2d 588 (1977), *aff'd sub nom.* American Tel. and Tel. Co. v. FCC, 572 F.2d 17 (2nd Cir.), *cert. denied*, 439 U.S. 875 (1978).

30. AT&T Long Lines Dept., 64 F.C.C.2d 959 (1977), *aff'd sub nom.* Aeronautical Radio, Inc. v. FCC, 642 F.2d 1221 (D.C. Cir. 1980), *cert. denied*, 452 U.S. 920 (1981).

31. MCI Telecommunications Corp. v. FCC (Execunet I), 561 F.2d 365 (D.C. Cir. 1977), *cert. denied*, 434 U.S. 1040 (1978); MCI Telecommunications Corp. v. FCC, (Execunet II), 580 F.2d 590 (D.C. Cir.), *cert. denied*, 439 U.S. 980 (1978).

32. Lincoln Tel. and Tel. Co. v. FCC, (Execunet III), 659 F.2d 1092 (D.C. Cir. 1981).

33. MTS and WATS Market Structure (CC Docket No. 78-72), 81 F.C.C.2d 971 (1977), *further recon.*, 67 F.C.C.2d 1441 (1978).

34. Resale and Shared Use, 83 F.C.C.2d 167 (1980).

35. AT&T (Docket 18128), 61 F.C.C.2d 587 (1976), *recon.*, 64 F.C.C.2d 971 (1977), *further recon.*, 67 F.C.C.2d 1441 (1978).

36. 642 F.2d 1221 (D.C. Cir. 1980), *cert. denied*, 451 U.S. 910 (1981).

37. Amer. Tel. & Tel. Co. (CC Docket No. 79-245), 84 F.C.C.2d 384, *recon.*, 86 F.C.C.2d 667 (1981), *aff'd sub nom.* MCI Telecommunications Corp. v. FCC, 675 F.2d 408 (D.C. Cir. 1982).

38. *See* United States v. Amer. Tel. & Tel. Co., 552 F. Supp. 131, 162 (D.D.C. 1982), *aff'd sub nom.*, Maryland v. U.S., 103 S.Ct. 1240 (1983).

39. Lincoln Tel. & Tel. Co., 72 F.C.C.2d 724 (1979).

40. MTS and WATS Market Structure, CC Docket No. 78-72, Phase III, FCC 83-178 (released May 31, 1983).

41. ENFIA stands for "Exchange Network Facilities for Interstate Access."

42. *See* Exchange Network Facilities, 71 F.C.C.2d 440 (1979). *See also* Exchange Network Facilities For Interstate Access, 90 F.C.C.2d 6 (1982), *aff'd sub nom.* MCI Telecommunications Corp. v. FCC, 712 F. 2d 517 (D.C. Cir. 1983).

43. MTS and WATS Market Structure, CC Docket No. 78-72, Phase I, Third Report and Order, FCC 82-579 (released February 28, 1983), *recon.*, 48 Fed. Reg. 42987 (1983) *appeal filed sub nom.* National Ass'n. of Regulatory Util. Comm'rs. v. FCC, D.C. Cir. No. 83-1225, et al. (March 1, 1983).

44. Competitive Common Carriers (CC Docket No. 79-252), First Report and Order, 85 F.C.C.2d 1 (1980).

45. Competitive Common Carriers (CC Docket No. 79-252), Second Report and Order, 91 F.C.C.2d 59 (1982), *recon. denied*, FCC 83-69 (released March 21, 1983).

46. Competitive Common Carriers (CC Docket No. 79-252), Fourth Report and Order, FCC 83-481 (released November 2, 1983).

47. Long-run Regulation of AT&T (CC Docket No. 83-1147), FCC 83-482 (released October 27, 1983).

4
THE MARKETPLACE

Economic Implications of Divestiture

by Robert W. Crandall and Bruce M. Owen[1]

In the late 1960s, the Federal Communications Commission (FCC)—with the prompting of academic opinion, the Department of Justice, and the courts—began to allow competitive entry into AT&T's regulated telecommunications monopoly, beginning with interstate microwave services and customer premises telephone equipment. By the mid 1970s, competitive entry had become very important as new carriers and equipment suppliers began to compete actively for markets that had been dominated for decades by AT&T, its operating companies, and the independent telephone companies.

Unfortunately, the FCC could find no effective way to regulate AT&T's response to competitive entry. Little importance had been attached historically to the problem of regulating individual AT&T tariffs. But with competitive entry into some service markets, the structure of individual tariffs became very important.

Obviously, entrants would first attack the markets in which prices were furthest above the cost of service. But how was AT&T to respond? Could it be allowed to slash selected tariffs without limit to repel the new entrants? If not, how would the Commission determine the depth of the allowable price cut?

Since AT&T operating companies controlled a large share of the local circuits connecting subscribers to the long-distance networks, new entry into local exchange service was not possible. Still, equipment suppliers and the new long-distance services competitors required connections to AT&T-owned local facilities in order to be able to compete. Equipment suppliers would have to assure their customers that the competitive equipment could be attached to AT&T local circuits, and the interexchange service companies required AT&T local circuits to reach their subscribers. In both cases, AT&T resisted FCC orders to interconnect with its new competitors.

The FCC was thus faced with two sets of issues: 1) how to regulate AT&T's competitive interstate rates, and 2) how to deal with demands for competitive access to AT&T's local circuits. On both issues, AT&T bought precious time by opposing regulatory proposals to liberalize access or to assess the cost basis for competitive prices. For some time, the FCC was not able to form a clear strategy in either area. Indeed, the Commission has still not discovered a method for measuring AT&T costs that would permit it to regulate effectively interstate rates or the terms of access to local facilities in a way that eliminates anticompetitive behavior. It may be that the problem is too difficult to admit to any practical regulatory solution.

In 1974, the Justice Department responded to the apparent success of AT&T's delaying tactics and the FCC's difficulties by filing an antitrust complaint against AT&T and Western Electric. The suit contended that AT&T had violated Sections 1 and 2 of the Sherman Act. This case was litigated through late 1981. As AT&T was concluding its defense, the parties reached a dramatic agreement on a consent decree to settle the case.

In this chapter, we review in summary terms the economic theory offered by the government and the appropriateness of the decree in light of this theory. We explore some of the ways that its theory could be applied to other situations, but note that it is not necessarily relevant to all regulated markets.

Our analysis of the decree includes a number of criticisms of its immediate impact as well as some concerns about the future effects of its provisions. Much of this analysis is speculative, for it is very difficult to predict the future course of technology or markets and regulatory developments in the numerous interrelated telecommunications markets. As a result, our conclusions are necessarily tentative but, we hope, provocative.

There is likely to be little interest in a paper that merely extolls the many virtues of the decree issued by Judge Greene. The reader should not interpret our criticism of certain features of the decree as a general condemnation of its provisions. On the contrary, the outcome of *United States v. AT&T* is very likely the most significant positive achievement in the 93-year history of Section 2 of the Sherman Act.[2] The settlement reflects great credit, in our view, on both parties and on Judge Greene.

ECONOMIC THEORY OF UNITED STATES V. AT&T

In this section, we outline the economic theory that motivated the government's case against AT&T.[3] This economic theory was stated in the pretrial pleadings and in testimony at trial. Judge Greene's August 1981 opinion denying AT&T's motion for dismissal reflects an acute understanding of the theory.[4]

The AT&T case was brought under the Sherman Act. The government claimed that AT&T had engaged in a course of illegal conduct for which the only effective remedy was divestiture from the AT&T holding company of the telephone operating companies.

From a legal point of view, of course, possession of a monopoly is not in itself illegal. But the acquisition and maintenance of a monopoly by *illegal* means does give rise to antitrust liability. As a result, the government had to prove that AT&T had engaged in various "bad acts," such as exclusionary pricing, in order to win its liability case.

From an economic point of view, the government had to show the link between these bad acts and AT&T's structure. Structural relief, such as divestiture, would be legally justified if it could show that AT&T had engaged in a pattern of illegal activity, the incentive and opportunity for which arose from its structure.

In addition, of course, the court had to consider the possibility that the structure of the company gave rise to *benefits* (e.g., economies of integration) that might outweigh the costs of monopoly. This analysis was undertaken privately by the Department of Justice in developing its relief proposal. The issues were to have been considered by Judge Greene at a separate post-trial relief proceeding if AT&T had lost the case.

AT&T defended itself in various ways. It denied that it had committed many of the "bad acts," or denied that the acts were bad. It claimed that monopoly was the best structure for the telecommunications industry, and that actions to preserve monopoly were therefore justified. It emphasized the legal theory that it was regulated, and therefore without market power and perhaps immune from antitrust liability.

The company produced various studies and economic experts claiming to show that it enjoyed economies of scale and high rates of productivity growth. It produced various military officers who praised AT&T's contribution to the national security.

AT&T also claimed, especially in the private antitrust cases, that it was the victim of inept and even malign government regulators. Judge Greene did not permit AT&T's lawyers to make personal attacks on these officials, but judges in some of the private actions permitted and even joined these attacks.[5]

Market Definition

The first step in most antitrust analyses is to define the relevant market. In a monopoly case, the line of business allegedly monopolized must constitute a proper economic market.

An economic market is a collection of products or services in a specified geographic area that, if offered by a single seller, would allow a profitable increase above competitive levels for a sustained period.

Market definition is often a hard-fought issue in antitrust cases. In *United States v. AT&T*, market definition was not a key issue, because AT&T pretty clearly had a monopoly in most areas no matter how the market was defined. Nevertheless, some aspects of market definition were vigorously litigated.

In general terms, the following areas were at issue in market definition:

- Long-distance services (ranging from ordinary telephone service to digital data services).
- Local telephone service.
- Telephone equipment used by customers (ranging from ordinary telephones to computerized private branch exchanges).
- Telephone equipment used by telephone companies.

Several of these categories represent a bundle of products or services, not a single market. But for purposes of analysis of AT&T's structure, these are convenient categories. AT&T generally provided long-distance services on a common set of facilities. Local telephone service consisted of a series of individual geographic monopolies, each owned by Bell.[6] The two equipment categories each consisted of various disparate types of equipment, usefully aggregated because treating each type individually would simply be repetitious.

The only really novel feature of the government's case with respect to market definition was its unsuccessful attempt to define a "Bell-only" market for equipment used by telephone companies. While Judge Greene rejected this market definition, he did find that the government had made out a *prima facie* case of market foreclosure with respect to such equipment.[7]

Vertical Market Foreclosure

The government's fundamental theory was based on the fact that the Bell operating companies possessed (legal) monopoly franchises providing local exchange service to most telephone customers. The argument was that Bell had used this control of "bottleneck" facilities to shut out long-distance competitors of AT&T Long Lines and equipment competitors of Western Electric.

The AT&T case must be distinguished from the case of vertical integration by an "ordinary" monopolist. In most instances, vertical integration does not carry with it any increased market power. That power is ordinarily fully exploitable in the original monopolized market from which the integration takes place. But there are exceptions to this; in practice there are various ways (other than cost savings) in which such integration may increase profits and/or market power. Sometimes, vertical integration can reduce welfare.

There does not seem to be any easy or intuitively satisfying way to summarize the conditions that distinguish harmful from benign vertical integration. Case by case analysis is required. Such integration may sometimes permit price discrimination among customers or suppliers. Foreclosure of an affiliate's competitor from part of its natural geographic market may, to take another example, create special cost advantages for the affiliate without substantially reducing the profits of the monopoly stage. Normally, in the case of fixed proportions, profits earned in this way could instead be earned simply by charging monopoly prices for access to the bottleneck. But there are special cases in which this must be done through vertical integration.

In the case of AT&T, the distinguishing feature was rate of return regulation. AT&T was, and still is, regulated by state and federal commissions that set an upper limit on its rate of return. If we assume that these limits are effective, AT&T must earn lower profits from its monopoly services than are available in the market.

Faced with the risk of competition, AT&T may react by lowering prices in the threatened markets and then seeking higher rates in other markets through proceedings before state and federal regulators. As long as regulators are unable to disentangle the costs of the various services, such a strategy can succeed up to the point at which the rates in the noncompetitive markets reach pure monopoly levels.

AT&T has an incentive to engage in such pricing behavior for a number of reasons. First, as long as it has the capital equipment in place, AT&T has the legitimate incentive to react to competitive thrusts by reducing rates toward variable costs. Some recovery of revenues for embedded plant is better than none at all. The problem is, as we discuss below, that AT&T has anticompetitive incentives to price even lower. The fact that it might subsequently seek rate increases in the "monopoly" services only serves to make such decisions easier.

Second, as long as regulators allow AT&T to earn more than a competitive return on invested capital, AT&T has an incentive to maintain its full network service. Over time, competition will reduce AT&T's market share and, therefore, its requirements for communications plants. Allowing itself to be reduced in scope by competition when incremental losses of market translate into lower capital requirements and, therefore, lower monopoly profits, is obviously not in the interests of AT&T.

Third, entry into telecommunications markets must be viewed as a sequential process. AT&T could restrict entry into interstate communications markets by denying access to local subscriber loops. By doing so for any single new service, it reduces the profitability of entry into other services, some of which have been extremely profitable to AT&T.

Prior to divestiture, AT&T had similar leverage with respect to competitors building national networks for a given service. By denying such competitors services that could be used to "piece out" the new networks during construction, AT&T could reduce its competitors' demand. Surely, it knew that if a new competitor developed transmission and switching capacity on major routes like Chicago-St. Louis or Washington-New York for the purposes of offering private-line services, that competitor would be poised to offer other services, such as television interconnection or switched message services. Eventually, these entrants would invade all of the major service markets on dense routes, severely reducing AT&T's cash flow in the short run and the size of the necessary AT&T plant in the long run.

Another method AT&T could have used to meet its regulatory constraint was to undertake activities increasing its own costs or reducing its own local revenues in order to hurt competitors. AT&T also had an incentive arising from regulation itself to export profits to its unregulated upstream subsidiaries. For example, AT&T could pay "too much" for equipment and thereby earn profits at Western Electric that regulators sought to prevent at the operating company level.

By virtue of its freedom in most areas from competitive pressure, AT&T was also in a position to take its "profits" in the form of higher costs, inefficiency, and excessive service quality. Its managers could, within limits, indulge not their preference for profits but rather a simple preference for monopoly and the "quiet life." All of these effects were theoretically inherent in AT&T's structure and in its regulation.

AT&T's actual use of bottleneck local exchange monopolies to foreclose competition or to disadvantage competitors was relatively easy to prove. In some cases, AT&T simply refused to interconnect at all with its early competitors such as MCI. In other cases, it refused to supply certain types of interconnections or restricted interconnection in ways that were deliberately inconvenient for competitors. The customer premises restriction (under which AT&T refused to interconnect with the specialized carriers at any point except the premises of mutual customers) is a good example of this.

In the equipment area, AT&T at first simply refused to supply service to customers that purchased non-Bell equipment. Later, AT&T insisted on an unnecessary "protective coupling arrangement" before it would interconnect with such equipment. Vendors of competing equipment were harassed by local operating company employees in other ways that made no sense except that Western Electric was affiliated with the operating company.[8] Even at low levels, AT&T employees were effectively indoctrinated to consider the interests of the company as a whole, not just the subsidiary that currently employed them.

But other categories of behavior were a good deal harder to prove, despite the presence of a valid economic theory predicting their occurrence. Take, for example, the issue of discrimination by Long Lines and the operating companies against outside equipment vendors. The theory that Western would be the preferred supplier did not mean that Western equipment would be chosen regardless of its relative cost and performance. Indeed, AT&T did buy some equipment from outside sources.

Proving a pattern of discrimination against outside vendors therefore often came down to the *ex post* evaluation of subjective comparative judgments. Testimony by former employees as to the spirit in which these subjective comparisons were made probably was the most effective evidence presented in this area.[9]

Cross-Subsidization and Exclusionary Pricing

Pricing issues presented by far the most difficult problems. The FCC began to authorize competition by MCI and the other specialized and domestic satellite carriers in the early 1970s. The new competitors were met with a series of price responses by AT&T: the Telpak tariff (a bulk discount on private lines that was in effect well before 1970), the Hi-Lo tariff, the MPL tariff, and the DDS tariff.

Each of these price responses appeared to be an attempt to exclude the new entrants, or in the case of the earlier Telpak tariff, to prevent customers from buying their own communications facilities. The developing antitrust law of *predatory* pricing has given such behavior a particular and rather narrow definition: first, pricing is set "below cost" in order to drive out or forestall entrants; later, prices are increased. The legal debate on predatory pricing has indeed narrowed even further to the issue of what particular definition of cost should be used in deciding whether price is below cost.

The difficulty in the AT&T case was that the costs of a particular service were difficult to determine because of the substantial common, or joint, costs in the AT&T system. The same facilities were used to provide a number of different services, and AT&T's FCC-mandated accounting system is not a very useful device for determining even the directly attributable costs of a particular service. Many "services" were not really distinct, but merely different names (and prices) for the same service. The same equipment and people produced both competitive and monopoly services, as well as local and long-distance service. The production decisions and all the relevant information were controlled by AT&T. Moreover, AT&T seemed to pay little attention to its costs in setting rates on competitive services.

AT&T's counsel and consultants later advocated long-run incremental, or Ramsey, pricing as a cost standard for pricing, while its competitors and the FCC advocated some form of fully allocated costs pricing. But the government alleged that in establishing some of its competitive tariffs, AT&T officials neither knew nor cared whether any of these standards were being met.

In any case, the government simply did not have any evidentiary basis for showing that AT&T's service prices were below cost, because neither the government nor (apparently) AT&T had any clear idea of what the costs were. Indeed, many of AT&T's competitive rates, such as Telpak, had been repeatedly declared unlawful by the FCC because of AT&T's failure to provide an adequate cost justification for them.

This difficulty led the government to abandon the attempt to prove that AT&T's service prices were predatory in the sense of being below cost. Instead, the government proposed to show that AT&T rates were evidence of AT&T's illegal *intent* to drive out or forestall competitors because they were set "without regard to costs." Rate of return regulation would permit such action to be consistent with profit maximization as long as the firm's overall return is not reduced below the level regulators allowed. In a regulated setting, anticompetitive intent seems the most likely explanation of a rational businessman's deliberate ignoring of cost in setting competitive prices.

"Pricing without regard to cost" is not a mysterious idea. A regulated monopolist offers two services, each priced (because of regulation) at less than profit-maximizing levels. The two services are provided using largely common facilities. One service accounts for more than 90% of total revenue and remains a monopoly. The other is subjected to competitive entry. The utility knows its overall costs and revenues.

Desiring to preserve its monopoly because it can thereby increase its profits, the company drops its price for the competitive service to a level calculated to drive out the entrants. In doing so, it disregards the cost (marginal, variable, or otherwise) of the service, in the expectation that any resulting short-term revenue losses can be recouped subsequently by seeking higher rates from regulators for the monopoly service.

But the revenue consequences of this pricing strategy are likely, in any event, to be a tiny factor in the overall revenues of the firm, and only one of many uncertain factors affecting future revenues. The utility can, and does, raise monopoly rates every few years because of inflation. In these circumstances, no fine calculations are needed to see that "pricing without regard to cost" is consistent with a "rational" intent to monopolize.[10]

Cross-subsidization took place or was alleged to take place in various ways within AT&T. Some of these cross-subsidies were admitted by Bell and even used as part of its defense. Generally, AT&T claimed that there were subsidies running to high cost rural, residential, and local service customers at the expense of lower cost urban, business, and long-distance customers. The government generally claimed that the complicated financial flows within AT&T resulted in subsidies from "monopoly" services to "competitive" services, and from local operating companies to Western Electric.

Neither side presented serious quantitative analyses of these issues for the reason already given: there was no practical basis for establishing the actual costs of the various categories of service, much less what the costs should have been, had managerial decisions been unbiased. Who can say, for example, whether the so-called "license fees" paid by the operating companies to AT&T for its and Bell Labs' services were above or below the levels that would have prevailed without any incentive on the part of the operating companies to help AT&T deal with its competitors?

The economic theory of the government's case against Bell is in many respects unique to the circumstances of AT&T. While it is possible to think of examples of other similar situations where it might apply, they are not common.

The first necessary condition for a case of this sort is that the monopolist control a "bottleneck" or an "essential facility." In the case of AT&T, the bottleneck was local exchange service required by long-distance competitors and equipment suppliers.[11] When the AT&T case was filed, no one doubted that local exchange service was a monopoly. As the years pass, new technologies raise the possibility that local exchange services may someday be provided competitively, enabling customers to "bypass" telephone company facilities.[12] It is possible that if the case had not been settled, its ultimate judicial conclusion and the advent of bypass might have been simultaneous events. But until bypass becomes reality, it is difficult to think of a better example of a bottleneck than a single firm in possession of a monopoly franchise operating the only feasible technology for serving the market.

A second necessary condition is that the bottleneck monopolist be vertically integrated into related businesses that are (or ought to be) competitively structured.

A third necessary condition (at least if one assumes profit maximization) is that there be some special mechanism, some leverage, or some feature of the market that permits the vertically integrated firm to translate or perfect its monopoly power in the bottleneck market. This last condition is very difficult to state in general terms. In the AT&T case, the special feature was regulation. But regulation probably is not the only mechanism that satisfies this condition. For example, AT&T might successfully have maintained its long-distance monopoly by refusing to interconnect with its competitors in a relatively small portion of the United States. This might well have fatally wounded the demand for its competitors' services (or raised their costs).

If these three conditions are met, it seems likely that there is a *prima facie* economic case that vertical integration will give rise to anticompetitive incentives and opportunities.

At this point, the analysis must turn to an evaluation of the benefits, if there are any, of the vertical integration in question. While AT&T produced many economists and econometric studies of economies of scale in its activities, it produced relatively little relevant evidence on economies of vertical integration.

In the end, there was little if any quantitative evidence either proving or disproving the existence of efficiency from AT&T's integration across the lines of the divestiture. One can make these inferences only from AT&T's failure to present such evidence and from AT&T's willingness to agree to divestiture. While such inferences are obviously risky, they are the only evidence available.

The Structure of Relief

In January 1982, nearly eight years after the filing of the complaint, the Justice Department and AT&T announced agreement on a decree that would settle the case. The relief was in all essential respects identical in form to that sought by the government at trial.[13] This relief was modified somewhat by Judge Greene, and the Modified Final Judgment (MFJ) was approved by both parties in July 1982.

The important provisions of the relief are:

- A requirement that AT&T divest itself of all of its operating companies.
- A requirement that the divested operating companies provide equal access to all interexchange carriers.
- Permission for AT&T to keep Long Lines, Western Electric, and Bell Laboratories.
- A prohibition on AT&T entry into electronic publishing.
- Retention by the operating companies of the right to sell or lease terminal equipment (but not the outstanding equipment, which remains with AT&T) and of the *Yellow Pages*.
- A repeal of the 1956 Consent Decree allowing AT&T to keep its patents and to provide unregulated services and equipment.

It was left to AT&T to decide how many groups of independent operating companies would be created and how big the local exchange areas would be.

Divestiture. The theory behind the divestiture of the operating companies was detailed above. Operating companies control the "bottleneck" of local access to subscribers. Hence, in the presence of binding regulation, they are likely to favor their own affiliated suppliers of interexchange service and equipment. Severing the local distribution function from interexchange services and equipment ends this vertical incentive to impede entry into the potentially competitive interexchange services and equipment markets.

The justification for this separation must be that any joint economies of providing local exchange and interexchange services are more than offset by the efficiency losses from Bell's Long Lines monopoly power in interexchange services and the one-time costs of the divestiture itself. As we have pointed out, there is virtually no evidence bearing on the existence of joint economies. Therefore, it would be very difficult to prove that the divestiture is necessarily welfare-enhancing.

The justification for divestiture must therefore lie either in the presumption that AT&T did not produce proof of these joint economies because they were non-existent or that the economies, if they exist, are outweighed by the benefits of increased competition.

Equal Access. The crux of the government's services case against AT&T involved the claim that the operating companies discriminated against Long Lines' competitors by providing the competition access to their local distribution systems on terms that were inferior to those offered to Long Lines. The decree specifies that the divorced operating companies provide equal access to all interexchange carriers.

There are two problems with this requirement that may make it difficult to enforce. First, access charges for interstate interexchange services are regulated by the FCC, while intrastate rates are regulated by the state commissions.

A second problem in assuring equal access derives from the variety of services required by various interexchange carriers. Given differences in customers, billing methods, service options, and equipment, each interexchange carrier may demand a unique set of services from the operating companies. It will be difficult to measure the differences in costs and value for these services. As a result, the "equal" access provisions may be impossible to enforce.

Removal of discrimination in access charges is therefore almost wholly dependent on divestiture removing the incentive for such discrimination. It does not do so, of course, for interexchange services within an operating company's own Local Access and Transportation Area (LATA).

Western Electric and Bell Laboratories. The MFJ allows AT&T to keep Bell Laboratories, Long Lines and Western Electric. The rationale for divesting these organizations from AT&T rested upon the relationships among themselves and with the operating companies. Western Electric maintained a large share of the telephone equipment and terminal equipment markets because of its affiliation with Long Lines and with the operating companies. Divestiture of the operating companies relieves them of their corporate loyalty to Western Electric. Of course, Long Lines will retain this loyalty, but the decree is founded on the proposition that sufficient competition among interexchange carriers will eventually develop and make the vertical integration between Long Lines and Western Electric harmless.

Divestiture of Western Electric was advocated as a means of preventing the Bell operating companies from helping Western monopolize equipment, as well as to prevent AT&T from using regulation to shelter inefficient manufacturing operations, and avoiding the strictures of rate of return regulation. An earlier antitrust action (settled in 1956) centered on the issue of whether this vertical integration allowed Bell to evade regulation by hiding its monopoly profits in Western Electric, an unregulated equipment supplier. With the development of competition in terminal equipment, AT&T could use regulation to cross-subsidize exclusionary behavior in the customer premises equipment market.

The divestiture of the operating companies makes cross-subsidies or regulatory avoidance less likely by removing the incentive of the operating companies to help Western maintain its monopoly. But if Long Lines has some regulated monopoly businesses, the incentive for exclusionary behavior by AT&T remains. The FCC's *Computer II* decision requires a separation of monopoly and competitive businesses within AT&T, but the MFJ does not.[14]

Similar considerations apply to Bell Laboratories. The AT&T operating companies provided much of the support for the Laboratories. But with divestiture, this support disappears. As a result, it is no longer possible for the operating companies to cross-subsidize Bell Labs' research, which in turn supports Western Electric product innovation and AT&T services generally.

Without general deregulation (and demonopolization) of interstate interexchange services, AT&T's continued ownership of Western Electric and Long Lines poses the same problems as vertical integration between Western and the operating companies once provided. Fortunately, it appears that most of Long Lines' business will be subject to rapidly increasing competition. But as long as the FCC (imperfectly) regulates the "dominant" interstate carriers' noncompetitive businesses, problems of vertically-related cross-subsidies remain.

Prohibition of AT&T Entry into Electronic Publishing.   The MFJ contains a provision that prevents AT&T from entering electronic publishing for seven years. This restriction was imposed by Judge Greene. It was not sought by the Justice Department.

While Judge Greene justifies the restriction in sweeping terms, suggesting that it will prevent AT&T from "crushing" small, new competitors in electronic publishing, the provision appears to be more related to political realities than competitive efficiency. This type of restriction had been sold in earlier years by the newspaper industry to the House Communications Subcommittee, and its political appeal is obvious. The Judge devoted 12 pages of his August 1982 opinion to this relatively minor issue.

Retention of Yellow Pages and CPE Sales/Rentals. In the original Justice-AT&T decree, *Yellow Pages* were to remain with AT&T, not the operating companies. This presumably reflects the Department's assessment that directory advertising is not a natural monopoly business.

Judge Greene reversed this decision in his August 1982 opinion, arguing that *Yellow Pages* would and should subsidize local telephone service. Since ownership of the local exchange network is not a requirement ("bottleneck") for directory publishing, he reasons, there was no possibility that the operating companies could use their local monopolies to cross-subsidize directory advertising. To allow AT&T to have this presently monopolized service would be counter to the spirit of the antitrust laws, according to Greene.

In addition to *Yellow Pages*, Greene also insisted on allowing the divested operating companies to sell or lease customer premises equipment (CPE) after first transferring the existing stock to AT&T. Greene argued that the operating companies would add to the vigor of competition in this market and that the risks of cross-subsidization are minor, because the operating companies will not produce the equipment. Greene also reasoned that the costs of providing local exchange service and vending customer premises equipment are so easily separated that regulators should be able to police cross-subsidies.

Both changes in the original proposed decree appeared to reflect a concern by Judge Greene that the adjustment to life without AT&T would be difficult for the operating companies. This concern reflects, probably, one of AT&T's major defenses against the lawsuit and against the introduction of competition.

AT&T argued for many years that local telephone rates were held down by subsidies from long-distance rates, a proposition many people believe. Opposition to the decree issued by Judge Greene came from those who believed that local rates would rise, or those who played on such fears.

Judge Greene appears to be giving the operating companies a source of revenues to ameliorate the adjustment problems (the necessity of raising local rates) without violating the spirit of the relief—namely, to separate competitive and monopoly services.

Enhanced Services. Finally, the decree essentially removes the anticompetitive 1956 restrictions upon AT&T that limited it to regulated communications services. AT&T is now permitted to offer hybrid communications-computer services and to enter the computer and electronics industries without restriction (except for "electronic publishing").

In 1980, the FCC essentially lifted the restrictions on such entry by AT&T in its *Computer II* decision. The FCC decision required AT&T to establish a separate subsidiary for all of its competitive businesses. The MFJ does not.

Computer II remains in effect, however, and the MFJ simply serves to reinforce the Commission's bold decision.

Questions Raised by the Decree

The implementation of the MFJ is not yet complete, but it raises a number of troubling questions for the future. Many of these questions center on the structure of the divested operating companies and their long-run viability. Without Judge Greene's modifications, these problems may have been more serious, but Greene's modifications create problems of their own.

In this section, we address a number of unanswered questions:

- Should Judge Greene have given *Yellow Pages* and the marketing of CPE to the operating companies?
- Is Judge Greene acting sensibly in his demarcation of the boundaries for LATAs?
- Should the operating companies be permanently prohibited from offering enhanced and other unregulated services?
- Is the issue of equal access treated too cavalierly in the decree?
- Should Judge Greene maintain jurisdiction indefinitely?[15]

Yellow Pages and CPE. Greene's decision to give the divested operating companies *Yellow Pages* and to allow them to market CPE are perhaps the two most controversial parts of his decision. They appear to run counter to the general approach of the decree—namely, the separation of monopoly and competitive services.

Greene's defense of allowing the operating companies to market CPE, as noted above, is that the opportunities to confound the regulators by assigning the costs of CPE marketing to local exchange service are limited. This may be true, but Judge Greene fails to note that state regulators have often been willing instruments of the local operating companies in their attempts to restrict competition in the terminal equipment market. As recently as 1974, the North Carolina Public Utility Commission sided with a small operating company in its battle against competitive sellers of terminal equipment.[16]

It is not clear that operating companies have traditionally subsidized local service using terminal equipment rentals. But some state commissions may believe that such subsidies are good public policy. If so, allowing the operating companies to continue offering "competitive" CPE may induce state regulators to encourage noncompetitive practices in setting local tariffs. In this way, the operating companies can earn supracompetitive rents on such equipment. That the operating companies may not manufacture such equipment does not appear to eliminate the problem.

The argument that CPE marketing and other operating company costs are readily segregated ignores the very substantial overlap in sales and overhead costs, each of which are likely to loom large in the new competitive environment. Marketing local exchange service and customer premises equipment is likely to require the same personnel and facilities. Overhead costs allocations are always arbitrary.

Finally, the opportunity to cross-subsidize among different types of CPE as well as between CPE and local exchange service cannot be ignored. Some "local exchange services" such as Centrex or Custom Calling are a direct substitute for terminal equipment. It may be hard to distinguish between the two.

Having offered the obvious criticism of Judge Greene's modification of the CPE provisions, we must offer a broader reflection. Telephone service is not the only regulated monopoly in the country. If a regulated firm can increase its supracompetitive profits by cross-subsidizing the sale of equipment vertically related to the regulated service, why have there been no similar problems for regulated firms in other markets? Electric utilities have not often attempted to control the market for devices (lamps, stoves, electric appliances) attached to their lines. Nor have gas utilities generally attempted to control the market for gas stoves or furnaces in their franchised areas.

On the other hand, gas pipelines have evaded regulatory constraint through vertical integration into gas field ownership.

Perhaps the absence of a national company, such as AT&T, offering local utility services, makes the profitable integration between equipment manufacture and local utility services less likely. Judge Greene's distinction between manufacture and marketing of CPE by operating companies may, therefore, have some validity. Otherwise, it is difficult to see how regulators would find it easier to prevent cross-subsidies in electricity, gas or water supply. In any event, the Department of Justice probably went too far when it said that it prefers "a complete prohibition on a regulated monopolist's provision of any competitive service."[17]

The *Yellow Pages* decision is in some ways more difficult to defend. Apparently, Judge Greene accepted the notion that *Yellow Pages* will necessarily earn supracompetitive profits for anyone who owns it. But he rejects the theory that this monopoly position derives from access to (and exclusion of others from) the operating company's telephone data base.

Rather than search for relief that would make directory advertising more competitive, he simply vests the monopoly service with the operating companies to cross-subsidize local service. But, if the operating company's data base is important, directory advertising will be less competitive than under alternate arrangements. Operating companies will have an incentive to block the entry of new directories if they own *Yellow Pages*, an incentive that would be lacking if *Yellow Pages* were offered by someone else.

It is not clear why it is desirable to increase competition in CPE by divorcing Western Electric from the operating companies but not desirable to effect the same result for directory advertising. Perhaps the Justice Department and the court believe that *Yellow Pages* advertising is a natural monopoly.

The Size Of LATAs. In carrying out the provisions of the MFJ, Judge Greene faced the difficult task of supervising the drawing of boundaries between local exchange and interexchange services. Specifically, boundaries were drawn to limit the geographical domain of each divested operating company's local exchange service. For this purpose, each LATA was crafted to define the limits of local exchange service.

AT&T proposed that its divested operating companies be organized into seven regional holding companies. These companies will provide local exchange service in 161 proposed LATAs, each generally the size of a large city and its surrounding rural areas. With certain modifications, Judge Greene approved this structure.[18]

The bottleneck natural monopoly local exchange service that was to be separated from competitive or potentially competitive interexchange service is defined in a peculiar way by the "LATA" concept. "Local exchange service" means, at a minimum, the twisted pairs of wires connecting customer terminal equipment to the local switch, as well as the switch, and whatever else needs to be included in order to minimize costs.

The "whatever else" included, in the original settlement, trunk connections up to Class 4 switching centers, at which operating companies would interconnect with long-distance companies. The revised concept permits the operating companies to go beyond this and offer long-distance toll service within LATAs.

Some of the proposed LATAs are quite large, at times covering an entire state. For instance, Nevada is a LATA. But Delaware is part of a LATA including Philadelphia, Pennsylvania. The argument in favor of large LATAs is that they provide greater revenue potential for the divorced operating companies. With small LATAs, many more calls are interexchange calls and, therefore, not available to the operating companies.

Large LATAs offer the Bell operating companies an opportunity to continue to monopolize a significant portion of toll service. States must approve intrastate intra-LATA toll entry and competition. There is a question concerning the degree to which intra-LATA tolls will be unbundled and priced separately from exchange access.

Obviously, establishing large LATAs to grant the operating companies a larger share of revenues transfers some services from a competitive to a regulated monopoly environment. The reason for the antitrust suit in the first place was to prevent local exchange monopolies from inhibiting competition in the long-distance market. Therefore, the larger the LATAs, the fewer the beneficial effects of the decree. This is especially important in states whose PUCs discourage intrastate competition.

It appears, however, that Judge Greene was concerned that smaller LA-TAs would result in the operating companies being left with the least advanced of AT&T's switching equipment. With limited inherited capital, they would be forced to invest *de novo* and might be more vulnerable to "bypass" technologies. This argument appears to be directed more to the transitional problems involved in divestiture than to the long-run problems of offering separate local exchange services.

At this stage of the divestiture proceeding, evaluating the LATA issue is difficult. Most of Judge Greene's discussion on the minimal efficient scale of local exchange service (or minimum hierarchical order for local exchange) is impressionistic at best. There is no easy answer to the question of what constitutes the minimum efficient size of a LATA. Even if there were an answer, it might change over time.

As a theoretical matter, an intra-LATA toll service is likely to give local operating companies an incentive to monopolize, engaging, if necessary, in cross-subsidization of intra-LATA toll services from the still monopolized exchange access services. Because it appears inevitable that regulators, courts, and legislators will sooner or later permit open entry into intra-LATA toll service, this is likely to cause continuing antitrust and regulatory problems. The potential for anticompetitive harm is ultimately limited, however, by the threat of bypass or the overpriced local exchange service itself.

Enhanced Services. The divorced operating companies are prohibited by the decree from offering enhanced or "information" services on the grounds that these services require access to the local distribution network. If the operating companies were allowed to compete in the market for these services, they would have the incentive and opportunity to cross-subsidize predatory thrusts from regulated local exchange service and to make access difficult for competitors.

While perfectly valid as far as it goes, this argument ignores the possibility that some undefined future "enhanced service" may yield real economies when offered by the operating companies.

Moreover, it seems unlikely that a restriction of operating companies to those services now called "local exchange" (and other regulated monopoly services) will enable them to be viable enterprises in future years. It is impossible to assume that technological change will not erode the local exchange service market or that joint economies in providing these and other services will never exist. To lock the operating companies into traditional local exchange services could well doom them to declining demand, reduced ability to attract capital, and a resulting decline in service quality.

On the other hand, permitting the operating companies to provide cellular radio telephone service may have been a serious error, delaying the advent of local service competition. Cellular radio provides a mechanism for competition with the local wireline service, rather than a lower-cost technology that might replace wireline service in the near future.

The Justice Department sued AT&T because it believed that the Bell operating companies had restricted the access of competing interexchange services and equipment suppliers to their local circuits. The decree reflects the government's (and Judge Greene's) view that divestiture is the appropriate relief in this case. However, there is no evidence that the new operating companies will be able to succeed in restricting enhanced services competition by denying access or cross-subsidizing. Until such evidence exists, no one can say whether it is desirable to restrict the operating companies to such a narrow range of services.

AT&T might have used its operating companies to restrict competition when firms such as Datran and MCI were major threats. But can one reasonably expect the divorced operating companies to successfully restrict competition by denying access to IBM, AT&T, or other large firms?

It is one thing to assume, on the basis of AT&T's failure to prove it, that there were no economies across the lines of the present divestiture. It is quite another to assume that there will never in the future be such economies in the joint provision of basic and enhanced services. Judge Greene could have restricted the operating companies from these markets for a brief period so that the practices of the past would not carry over to the future. But a ban on such entry appears to be based upon very strong assumptions about the prospects for anticompetitive behavior, perhaps based on nothing more or less than AT&T's historical intransigence to competition.

The operating companies are, of course, free to petition the court to modify the ban. But the outcome of this procedure is difficult to predict.

Equal Access for Interexchange Carriers.   The government's case relied very heavily upon the AT&T operating companies' failure to grant equal access to competitors of Long Lines. Judge Greene's decree remedies this past sin by divesting the operating companies and requiring them not to discriminate among interexchange carriers in the future.

But how is such a provision to be enforced? Unless all carriers require precisely the same services from the divested operating companies, difficulties in determining whether access is equal or equivalent will continue.

The attractiveness of the interexchange service market—either as an arbitrageur or as an owner of transmission and switching facilities—is a powerful reminder that the FCC has been unable or unwilling to regulate AT&T effectively. It cannot separate AT&T's costs despite decades of trying. Simply transferring the problem to the divested operating companies and specifying that all interstate carriers should be provided "equal access" will not solve the problems confronted by regulators.

Measuring the costs of access for different carriers will be no easier than distinguishing the costs of Telpak from those of WATS. Local operating companies share many of the same aspects of AT&T's operations that so confused regulators: common costs, joint costs, different vintages of equipment, different configurations of equipment to supply the same services, etc. How will the FCC or the state commissions enforce equal access charges given these cost accounting problems?

It is even possible that the state commissions will not wish to set equal access charges (for given quality interconnection) for interexchange carriers. As long as the operating companies retain some monopoly power in local exchange services, they may find it attractive to discriminate on access charges. State commissions will often be supportive of such discrimination because it can cross-subsidize the basic monthly household service charge.

Operating companies will obviously try to set the highest charges for those customers with the most inelastic demand for access, i.e., those with the most limited bypass options. The FCC's decision to assign the non-usage sensitive portion of local exchange costs to the subscriber has limited the scope for such discrimination. But it has not eliminated it.[19] As a policy matter, some discrimination may be a useful short term measure to aid the transition to cost based local access rates.

The Court's Continuing Supervision.   Judge Greene has declared that he will maintain jurisdiction over the enforcement of the decree indefinitely. Citing the complexity and magnitude of the case, he argues that the court must be prepared to take appropriate actions to ensure that the decree is executed properly and that the objectives of the decree are realized.

We see danger in indefinite close judicial supervision of this industry. The divestiture, new technologies, a surge of new entrants, and the visible nature of local subscriber rate regulation will combine to create substantial pressures for a variety of rates and new service options. The continuing jurisdiction of the federal court will give those damaged by competitive thrusts an easy avenue for appeal of marketplace dictates. Moreover, the court's continuing jurisdiction will provide future opportunities for judicial intervention that would not normally occur.

Judge Greene is an uncommonly astute and hard-working jurist, with life tenure. But the MFJ will outlive him. The purported benefits of the MFJ are those of enhanced service and rate competition. Continued judicial supervision of the decrees may impede the operation of these market forces, as it has, for example, in the *Paramount* decrees.

Extending the Theory to Other Cases

The AT&T decree is important not only for its impact upon telecommunications markets. The case has a number of important implications for antitrust enforcement policy. Applying the theory of the case to other antitrust problems is illustrated by two very recent cases: General Telephone's acquisition of Southern Pacific Communications (SPCC) and Ted Turner's lawsuit against Westinghouse.[20]

General Telephone (GTE) owns a number of telephone operating companies that provide monopoly local exchange service in various areas scattered throughout the United States. Southern Pacific Communications is the second largest of AT&T's new long-distance competitors.

The acquisition, in principle, creates precisely the problem that motivated the Bell breakup. The Department of Justice, however, has permitted the acquisition, provided that SPCC is kept in a "totally separate subsidiary" from GTE operating companies. The rationale is that, in the case of GTE, the separate subsidiary device may be an effective means of detecting and policing cross-subsidies because the two operations have never been integrated. The proposed GTE consent decree prohibits common facilities and common employees.

Thus, in the case of GTE/Sprint, the analysis of the economic effects of vertical integration are not qualitatively distinguishable from those of *U.S. v. AT&T*. But the analysis of relief is different for reasons based on the factual circumstances. For example, GTE is presently integrated with the AT&T/Independent "partnership," and will continue for some time to discriminate in favor of the partnership and against its own subsidiary, SPCC.

The GTE/SPCC acquisition raises some rather obvious questions about the continuing ban on former Bell operating companies reintegrating into long-distance and other competitive services, especially outside their own territories. One possible antitrust problem with such reintegration is the Bell central staff organization that will "coordinate" the operating companies.

Our description of the Turner lawsuit against Westinghouse will be based on stylized facts because the lawsuit was only recently filed. Westinghouse owns a chain of cable television systems (the former Teleprompter company), one of which is in Manhattan. Turner owns CNN, a 24-hour satellite news service that is sold to cable systems and broadcast stations. Westinghouse began its own 24-hour satellite news service and, according to Turner, discriminated against Turner's CNN on some of the Westinghouse cable systems in favor of its own vertically integrated service, Group W.

The two analytical issues are, first, whether cable is a bottleneck or essential facility for CNN, and second, whether Westinghouse can expect to profit from its action in a way that provides it with special incentives to integrate vertically and to monopolize the relevant upstream market. We can not dispose of these questions here, but merely outline some of the analysis.

First, the television industry is rapidly becoming deconcentrated as a result of FCC actions licensing domestic broadcast satellites, permitting low-power TV stations, and deregulating cable television. Moreover, the marketplace for alternative links between programmers and viewers has increased with video cassettes, disks, and the growth of independent TV stations.

Nevertheless, it is hard to see any of these avenues providing much of an alternative in the very short run to cable distribution for CNN. Furthermore, the short run may be critical, as it generally is for companies in a start-up period. So, depending on the facts, there may be a case that, at least with respect to CNN cable, is today a bottleneck with special access obligations under the antitrust laws.

A more difficult question is whether Group W's vertical integration into 24-hour news programming gives it a special incentive to discriminate against CNN. There is no rate-of-return regulation in cable. What profit can Westinghouse gain from discriminating against Turner that would not be available simply by charging higher prices to all for access to its systems?[21]

One possibility is that Westinghouse, by limiting the market to competitors of its news service, even for a relatively small fraction of the potential audience, may provide itself with a decisive competitive advantage because of the economies of spreading program costs over large audiences, and of selling larger audiences to advertisers. If so, Westinghouse might gain more profit from monopolizing the upstream program markets in which it operates than it loses in revenues from access charges at the local level. This dynamic mechanism would substitute for the role of rate-of-return regulation in the AT&T case.

Finally, there is a very substantial question as to whether 24-hour satellite news service is a "market" in the antitrust sense. If it is not, then Westinghouse would have no incentive to monopolize it and therefore no incentive to discriminate against it.

We do not wish, on the basis of hypothetical and stylized facts, to prejudge the merits of the Turner lawsuit. But we do want to point out that it has analytical similarities to *U.S. v. AT&T*. The lesson here and the lesson from GTE/SPCC is that the underlying principles of *U.S. v. AT&T* are likely to have continuing applicability in the future.

THE FUTURE OF COMPETITION IN TELECOMMUNICATIONS

The divestiture of the Bell operating companies from AT&T marks the end of the regulated *de facto* monopoly era in telecommunications. We are now entering a period characterized by intense competition among long-haul communications networks. While AT&T will continue for a time to dominate this marketplace, its share is likely to diminish.

There is no reason to conclude that AT&T is an efficient and skillful competitor. It has little experience in responding to customer needs in a timely way, and it would be surprising to find that AT&T (or its operating companies) has learned to minimize the cost of providing the services that it offers. Moreover, AT&T is likely for some time to face regulatory hurdles not confronting its competitors.

Continued regulation of AT&T is perhaps an idea whose time has passed. True, AT&T will continue to have some monopoly services and some market power, even though each will diminish. But the FCC has not been particularly successful in protecting either customers or competitors from the exercise of this power. And regulation, used so frequently by AT&T in the past to ward off competitors and perpetuate its monopoly, may now be the ironic instrument that chokes off AT&T's legitimate competitive responses to the new environment. One could argue that the world might be better off if the FCC had abolished common carrier regulation of AT&T (as opposed to the operating companies) on the same day that the divestiture took place, or soon after.

Whatever happens to Long Lines, the future of long-distance telecommunications seems, quite predictably, to be growth and increased competition. The really interesting battles will take place on bypass issues in the area of local exchange service. The outcome is very hard to predict.

Bypass takes two generic forms. In the first, long-distance services run their "lines" (whether wires, fibers, or radio links) directly to the customers' locations. This is obviously an attractive possibility with satellites. The customer and the carrier each bypass local exchange access fees, provided the call does not go to a non-subscribing party. This type of bypass will likely be relatively attractive to large customers.

The second type of bypass is the provision of local service itself by technologies other than local subscriber loops. Cellular radio and coaxial cable television systems are the most obvious technologies for this type of bypass. As we have already noted, Judge Greene and the FCC seem to have very different expectations about the imminence of bypass. Cable television systems and telephone companies are already fighting over federal legislation affecting the terms on which cable systems could provide local exchange services. State PUCs are becoming battlefields where long-distance companies and operating companies fight over complex access pricing issues. The local service area will be, we expect, a rich source of controversy in the years ahead.

NOTES

1. The authors are grateful to Peter Greenhalgh, Richard Levine, Roger Noll, Jeff Rohlfs, and Steve Zecola for useful comments and advice, but retain responsibility for errors.

2. The dismissal, on the same day, of the government's lawsuit against IBM may be the second most significant event.

3. There were also a number of private cases brought by AT&T competitors for treble damages. These generally involved some subset of the facts in the government case.

4. *See* the government's pretrial brief, dated December 10, 1980, pp. 23–26; Judge Greene's opinion is reported at 524 F. Supp. 1336 (1981).

5. Southern Pacific Communications Company v. AT&T, F. Supp. 825 (1983) and 913–14, 1056–58, 1097.

6. There are independent local telephone companies, but Bell operating companies embrace approximately 80 percent of all local telephone customers.

7. United States v. AT&T, 524 F. Supp. 1336, 1377–80 (1981).

8. Of course, in the absence of Western, the operating companies might have wanted to monopolize customer premises equipment sales on their own behalf.

9. Mr. William Browne, formerly an AT&T official in charge of facilitating sales of non-Bell equipment, testified for the government about the difficulties he encountered.

10. *See contra*, Brock and Evans, "Predation," in D.S. Evans, ed., *Breaking Up Bell*, North Holland 1983, 51–54 and 220–226.

11. AT&T's long-distance network was also, at least in the beginning, an essential facility for competitors to "piece-out" their incomplete networks.

12. But see Judge Greene's view that this is not imminent in his April 20, 1983 opinion on LATA boundaries.

13. It later developed that the parties' definition of "local exchange" was somewhat different from earlier understandings. See the discussion below of Local Access and Transportation Areas (LATAs).

14. The separate subsidiary approach was regarded by the Antitrust Division as an ineffective remedy in the case of AT&T. The Division has, however, now accepted that approach in distinguishable circumstances. *See* the discussion of the GTE/ SPCC acquisition below.

15. These are not the only problems with the decree. For instance, the Department of Justice seems to have missed an important opportunity to encourage bypass competition in local exchange areas by permitting the operating companies to retain the right to provide cellular mobile telephone service.

16. *See* North Carolina Utils. Comm'n. v. FCC, 552 F.2d 1036 (4th Cir.), *cert. denied*, 434 U.S. 874 (1977).

17. 48 Fed. Reg. 22033 (1983).

18. U.S. v. AT&T, et al., 569 F. Supp. 990 (1983), April 20, 1983.

19. Judge Greene has criticized this FCC action, apparently because he views it as inconsistent with his solution to the problem of local service rates going up "as a

result of the decree." Judge Greene's solution is to impose access charges on the long-distance companies using the local exchange services. The FCC and the operating companies fear this will encourage "bypass" of local facilities, with further adverse revenue consequences for the operating companies.

20. *See* DOJ Competitive Impact Statement in U.S. v. GTE, 48 Fed. Reg. 22020 (5/16/83). Turner's lawsuit was filed March 3, 1983 in Atlanta: Cable News Network v. Satellite News Channels and Westinghouse Broadcasting and Cable, (Case No. 83-430, N.D. Georgia, Atlanta Div.).

21. In fact, Westinghouse now pays CNN for service, rather than the reverse, while the Westinghouse service depends wholly on advertising revenues. This factual situation complicates the problem of proving or disproving "discrimination" without really changing the theoretical analysis.

5
TECHNOLOGY

The Anchor of the Bell System

by Charles L. Jackson

Anchors protect ships from the tides, currents, and storms. Historically, the Bell System's mastery of technology protected it from antitrust action and from competition.

Dragging anchors hold ships back. Today, changing technology, coupled with uneconomic depreciation policies, threatens to turn Bell's historical technology into a dragging anchor which will forever handicap the separated parts of the Bell System in their competitive struggles.

This chapter looks at technology from two points of view. First, it examines how the Bell System managed technology in the past in order to meet both political and economic objectives. Second, it considers the impact of changing technology on the spun-off components of the Bell System. Finally, it looks to the future of Bell Labs—the R&D arm of the Bell System.

BELL LABS

Bell Labs is a unique institution. Half owned by AT&T and half by Western Electric, it was the first major industrial research institution. Bell Labs is generally regarded as the world's best single research institution in communications and electronics.

A key question about the divestiture is the future of Bell Labs. Will the Labs prosper or decline in the new environment? Will they continue to add to our national wealth and productivity, or will they enter into a long period of decline?

Bell Labs came into being in 1925 with a staff of 3,600.[1] By the standards of those times, or by the standards of today, Bell Labs was massive at its birth. Nominally, the Labs served as the R&D arm of the Bell System. In fact, the labs were essentially the R&D arm of Western Electric—a manufacturing company. Their focus was always on communications technology and on the physical science underlying that technology. Because of this focus and because of the isolation of Western Electric from the competitive market, the Labs could invent the transistor and could bring out Picturephone without doing any market research.

The Role of Technology in AT&T's Dominance

Prior to 1945, Western Electric had the lion's share of the electronics market in this country. In 1930, Western Electric's sales equalled those of the rest of the electronics industry in the United States.

Western Electric's relative size and position in the electronics industry is also illustrated by a comparison with IBM. In 1940, Western's sales of $241 million were five times larger than IBM's sales of $46.3 million. By 1960, IBM's sales of $1.8 billion roughly matched Western Electric's sales that year of $2.6 billion worth of goods.

Recently, in 1982, IBM's sales of $40 billion dwarfed Western Electric's sales of $12.6 billion in that year. In 40 years, IBM grew 20 times more than did Western Electric. Yet at the same time, and by every measure, IBM's share of the data processing and computer market dwindled. Also over that period, the Western Electric/Bell Labs combination's relative position in the electronics industry shrank enormously—even though both organizations grew in absolute size.

If, roughly speaking, firms invested in R&D in proportion to sales, then Western/Bell Labs would in 1925 have outspent by two times the rest of the industry combined. With reasonable management, Bell could have been assured a commanding position in all areas of the new electronics technology. No firm could have challenged it in communications. And, in fact, Bell was technically preeminent because it owned the patents controlling most of the key technologies. Bell Labs was designed to see that such technological supremacy continued. But, as the electronics industry grew, it became harder and harder for the Labs to dominate research in electronics and communications.

But to explain Bell Labs as merely a tool that the Bell System could use against competitors is too easy. Bell Labs served other institutional norms and political needs as well.

Institutional Norms: Excellence and the Spirit of Service

One of the strongest and noblest of the Bell System's traditions is the "Spirit of Service" which emphasizes telephone service as service to the community rather than just another business. The lineman working outside during a storm or the operator staying at the switchboard during a flood are in the best tradition of the "Spirit of Service." Bell Labs—in its continuing attempts to reduce the cost and improve the reliability of communications— served this norm. Similarly, the Bell System possessed an excellence norm— one which Bell Labs fits well.

Both of these norms played major roles in Bell's success. As long as the United States had the world's best telephone system, Bell was relatively immune to antitrust actions motivated only by its size. As long as Bell dominated telecommunications and electronics technology, it was essentially immune to competition.

Bell's Position in the Electronics Industry

Electronics is a powerful and versatile technology. It can be used for entertainment, defense and computation as well as for telecommunications. World War II, the Cold War, and the space race each resulted in enormous expenditures on electronics and communications technology by the U.S. government. The Defense Department paid for the development of many of the early computers, for the development of microelectronics (integrated circuits were first used extensively in the Minuteman I and in some government communications systems), and for the development of highly advanced communication systems. This government research helped non-Bell organizations (e.g., Hughes, IBM, Motorola) build extensive technical capabilities in technologies key to the development of modern communication systems.

During the same period, the market for electronics grew explosively. Computers and home entertainment systems—especially television—increased to the point where they accounted for a larger share of the electronics industry than did Western Electric.

Thus, it is fair to say, by 1956—the year of the first AT&T consent decree—Bell Labs and Western Electric no longer controlled or dominated the pace and direction of innovation in communications and electronics. Read together with the Communications Act of 1934, the 1956 decree envisioned a world much like the then-recent past. AT&T and Western Electric would restrict themselves to the regulated telephone business. State and federal entry controls would keep competitors out of the telecommunications industry.

Bell was also required to cross-license its technology with others, a requirement essentially affirming existing practice. For example, Bell Labs held a series of transistor seminars in the early 1950s which taught firms such as Texas Instruments and Sony how to build and use transistors.

But, of course, the world of the 1956 decree was unstable. The newly developing computer industry needed communications equipment, especially modems and digital transmission links, which Bell was slow to supply.

Further, the spread of technology gave others the capability to build and use microwave radios and communication satellites.

Naturally enough, individuals and companies came forward to build competing networks and to interconnect non-Bell equipment to the network. Ultimately, notwithstanding the nominal bars to entry in the 1934 Act, these new entrants to the industry were allowed to proceed, albeit with limits at first. Specialized carriers were expected to offer private line service only, not switched voice telephone service.

Terminal equipment interconnection was limited and restricted. But, these restrictions gradually eroded.[2] Today, the only market where regulators still effectively limit entry is the metropolitan or regional signal distribution market.

THE FUTURE

Given Bell's current investments, our knowledge of the underlying technology and of the expected changes in that technology, what can we predict for the future of the separated elements of the Bell System? Forecasting the future is always a chancy business; the many uncertainties surrounding the future of the parts of the Bell System make forecasting their future especially difficult.

As I see it, the key controlling element is not technology, but whether or not the people of the reorganized Bell System can cope with their new roles.

The closing line of a recent article by two of Bell Labs' computer scientists stated: "A good product can find its way without marketing; indeed it may be the better for having no marketing concerns to drive it."[3]

If that attitude controls the behavior—or even significantly influences the behavior—of the enterprises spun off from the Bell System, then their future is bleak indeed. As shown below, most of the Bell System's offspring must live in competitive markets. And, as technology improves, all can be expected to face competition.

Contrast the view quoted above with the following:

> I was absolutely amazed at the number of engineers who were interviewed for jobs on the development side who wanted to meet the marketing guy. They wanted to have some assurance that the zippy ideas that were running around in their heads were going in fact to get marketing push. Now where do you find that elsewhere?[4]

This is the attitude of the highly competitive electronics industry which is one of AT&T's major competitors.

Market by Market Analysis

Bell's major markets today can be broken into the submarkets shown below:

Hardware:
- Components
- Switching Systems
- Transmission Systems
- Customer Premises Equipment

Services:
- Intercity voice
- Local (intracity) voice.

These markets will be pursued by different entities as shown below:

Hardware:
- Western Electric—Components
- Western Electric—Switching Systems
- Western Electric—Transmission Systems
- ATT-IS, Western Electric, The BOCs—Customer Premises Equipment

Services:
- AT&T—Intercity voice
- BOCs—Local (intracity) voice.

Components. Nuts, bolts, transistors, integrated circuits—these components are the basic building blocks of electronic systems. Components range from carbon resistors to advanced microprocessors—the computer on a chip. The component market can be divided into two sectors. The first is older, simpler components—such as carbon resistors—which are well understood, and are very much a commodity product. The second is comprised of newer, high technology products—such as microprocessor chips—which are more differentiated products and are harder to produce.

Historically, Western Electric has made many of the components which went into its own products. From the outside, the competitiveness of their components appears to be mixed. It appears that they are high-cost producers of some of the older, commodity components.

I predict that Western will not try to compete in these markets; if it does, it will do poorly. I expect that Western Electric will turn increasingly to the market to acquire many of these older technology components and will redirect the assets currently devoted to manufacturing these products.

Western Electric is among the world leaders in advanced semiconductor components.[5] It has announced the sale of 256K bit RAM chips to the trade in the fall of 1983. If they meet that deadline, they will probably be the first firm to offer the 256K Ram, the successor to the 64K RAM.

Success in this market has important economic, political and institutional impacts. Currently, the 64K RAM industry is dominated by the Japanese who have a 70 percent share of the worldwide market. Not to be outdone, the Japanese have also targeted the 256K RAM market.[6]

Western Electric is actively exploring the anti-Japan theme in advertising for the 256K RAM. A victory by Western Electric over Japan Inc. would legitimatize Western Electric's entry into the non-Bell markets in a way competition with domestic rivals never could. Of course, should they be successful in this market, they will be taking business away from domestic firms as well as from the Japanese.

The worldwide market for 256K RAMs is projected to grow to almost $4 billion per year by 1990.[7] Western Electric may be able to gain a significant share of this market if they are first to enter the market, keep their costs down, and market aggressively. Success here might, in turn, allow Western Electric to develop the market experience and reputation necessary to become a significant factor in much of the semiconductor industry. Western Electric and Bell Labs—home of the invention of the transistor—already have the necessary knowledge of the underlying technologies. And, a success here should have positive effects on the organization as well by showing that success in competitive markets is possible.

Switching and Transmission Equipment. Western Electric is the world's largest manufacturer of telephone switching and transmission equipment. Western Electric currently knows its switch and transmission customers well. Modern switches (central office switching machines) require massive computer programs to run them. They are essentially complex computers which must be compatible with the other computers (switches) in the communications network. The requirement for extremely expensive software development, the need for compatibility with the rest of the network, and the existing contacts between Western Electric and its customers (the BOCs and AT&T) all serve to make this market difficult for others to penetrate. Western Electric should do well in this market for at least a decade or two.

Transmission equipment (microwave radios, cables, modulators) tends to have standardized, simple interfaces. Furthermore, failure of a transmission link does not have the disastrous effect that the failure of a switch has. Thus, operating companies can easily experiment with various vendors of transmission equipment. Entry into this market is far easier for Western Electric's competitors than into the switching market. Thus, it will be a more competitive market, and Western can be expected to lose its market share here. Only if they become a low-cost producer can they expect to maintain a major market share.

Customer Premises Equipment (CPE). This is an awkward term. It refers to equipment such as telephone instruments, computer terminals, and switchboards (PBXs) which are located at the customer's facility. Participation of the separated parts of the Bell System in this market is complex. AT&T is allowed to sell CPE through its separate subsidiary, AT&T Information Systems (ATT-IS). Western Electric may manufacture CPE to be sold through ATT-IS. ATT-IS can also sell other manufacturers' CPE. As of January 1, 1984, the BOCs can sell—but not manufacture—CPE.

Under the current rules, the CPE market is wide open. No regulatory barriers to entry exist. This market will produce a real horse race. ATT-IS (AT&T's marketing arm) has an established presence with most customers. If they offer competitive products, they should be able to keep many of them.

Western Electric faces a more difficult problem. They must sell to ATT-IS. If Western Electric's products are not competitive in a particular line, ATT-IS can be expected to turn to outside suppliers. Otherwise, ATT-IS would be committing itself to self-destruction. Indeed, ATT-IS already uses outside (non-Western Electric) sources for several products.

Intercity Voice. The intercity voice market became AT&T's largest single revenue source on January 1, 1984—the day of divestiture. The provisions of the Modified Final Judgment (MFJ) giving the other intercity common carriers (MCI, SBS, Sprint[GTE]) "equal access" to customers will tend to turn long-distance service into a "commodity"-like product where customers choose the least expensive vendor.

There will be some difference in quality among the various vendors. For example, SBS's service will have the delay associated with satellite transmission. Intercity voice will become a highly competitive market with profits going to the low-cost supplier.

Local Voice. Local signal distribution will be the province of the BOCs. It is the only part of the traditional Bell System markets which remains a technical and regulatory monopoly. Yet, local signal distribution won't remain a technical monopoly for long. Alternative local signal distribution technologies—microwave radio, cellular mobile radio, and cable television plant—are now practical for use by large customers. While they are still too expensive for use in small businesses or in homes, a major cost for such systems is electronics—and the cost of electronics is dropping rapidly. It won't be long before alternative local distribution services make economic sense for many small businesses and residences.

Right now, the use of alternative local distribution systems is essentially restricted to two uses: access to long-distance services and intra-organization communications. I know of no case of a competitive system offering local switched voice service in competition with the local telephone company. But, private systems are being built on high density routes in the local area in a fashion parallel to the development of long haul private microwave systems in the 1950s and 1960s.

Furthermore, several firms have received FCC permission to offer a switched data service using microwave radio for local signal distribution.[8] The architecture of these systems allows them to offer local service—although regulators may try to prevent such use.

Some cable television systems are beginning to offer two-way data services. Two cable systems (Cable America in Atlanta and Cox in Omaha) have announced plans to offer local voice service between MCI's network and MCI's customers. Right now, however, cable television only reaches about 60 percent of households, and most cable systems do not have two-way capability. But it is a reasonable projection that the cost of the electronics necessary to transmit voice over a cable system will drop with an expansion of the market and with continued progress in electronics.

Essentially, all residential customers lack an alternative to the local telephone company today. Larger business customers have an alternative for some of their traffic, but they need the local telephone company to place local calls.

The telephone industry is trying to use the political process to slow down the growth of competitive local distribution systems. They have opposed legislation which would allow cable companies easier entry into the local data and voice markets. They have supported regulatory restraints on cable companies by state regulators. In one particularly flagrant case, the local telephone company unilaterally refused to continue allowing the cable company access to its poles and ducts.

Despite the telephone companies' opposition, I predict that alternative local distribution systems will grow in competition with the local telephone companies. The major conflict will come when the alternative local distribution systems begin to offer switched local voice services. At that point we will see a replay, in 50 states, of the conflict between Bell and the specialized carriers in the 1970s.

Bell Labs will survive the transition imposed on it, but it will be difficult and painful. Without a doubt, the nature of the Labs will change. The Labs will be forced closer to Western Electric and will come to be perceived more as the R&D arm of Western Electric than as an independent research institution. If Western shrinks from its present size, it will have a hard time paying for Bell Labs—the Labs are too big for a $6 billion a year manufacturing company. Thus, if Western shrinks, the Labs will probably have to shrink as well.

Still, the Labs will survive. It has a critical mass of first-rate scientists and engineers. Both AT&T and Western Electric need the inventions and computer programs that flow from it. If the Labs did not exist, Western Electric would have to create it. IBM has its Watson Labs and Xerox has its Xerox Parc (Palo Alto Research Center)—both world class research facilities.

DEPRECIATION

Depreciation policy—the rules regulators and accountants use to determine when consumers are charged for construction of a telephone plant—is an important, but obscure, corner of the communications world. Depreciation policy is tied to technology in two ways. First, the rate of technical change determines, in part, the true rate of economic depreciation of communications plant. Second, the depreciation rates allowed by regulators play a major role in the willingness and ability of communications companies to invest in new technology.

This section looks at the issue of depreciation policy for the communications industry. It reaches a simple conclusion—the old depreciation policies served us well in a period of monopoly and of slower technical change. However, the old policies are counter productive and even dangerous today. Still, moving to better depreciation policies requires a transition period with higher telephone rates than at present.

Depreciation, or "capital recovery," is a long name for a simple concept. Any business which has to set prices to recover costs faces a special problem whenever it acquires a long-lived piece of equipment. How should it spread the costs of this new piece of equipment over its customers?

Consider a newspaper which purchases a new printing press that will last for ten years. It would not be sensible to try to recover the costs of that printing press all in the first year—that might cause newspaper costs to double for 12 months and then reduce for nine years. The newspaper should apply the costs of the printing press evenly over the useful lifetime of the press. Applying one-tenth of the cost over each of ten years fairly reasonably reflects the costs of the printing press.

Charges for regulated utility service—including telephone service—have always included a component reflecting capital recovery or depreciation. In the telephone industry, these charges have always been quite low. The low charges were justified and were sound policy for many reasons. Telephone equipment must be reliable—we cannot afford to have the telephone quit working. But reliable equipment also lasts a long time—20 to 40 years for telephone equipment.

Depreciating equipment over long lifetimes kept phone rates down and helped spread universal telephone service. In a monopoly environment, the telephone company and the regulators could always count on being able to recover depreciation charges—to recover invested capital somehow. In the monopoly environment of the past, the physical lifetime and the economic lifetime of the equipment were the same.

The combination of rapid technical change and competition in telecommunications makes the old depreciation policies—based on the physical lifetime of equipment—obsolete. Almost everyone is familiar with the rapid fall in the price of pocket calculators after they were introduced in the early 1970s. The prices of calculators, computers, and many other electronic systems fall more quickly than the machines wear out. Last year's million-dollar computer is next year's half-million-dollar computer.

The economic depreciation of communications hardware must be measured by the cost of replacement hardware as well as by the physical lifetime of the hardware. In a competitive market, there isn't really any choice. If a telephone company depreciates an investment too slowly, there is no apparent problem at the beginning. But, services using the investment are being sold below cost. Later, when technical change has lowered the cost of new hardware, the depreciation charges will remain the same.

Services using the investment are now being sold above the cost of competitive services which use newer hardware. At that point, the telephone company is in a difficult bind indeed. It can cut its prices to match competition—but when it cuts prices it loses the opportunity to recover its investment. Essentially, the telephone company subsidized the earlier users of the service who obtained below-cost service. If the telephone company does not cut prices, then it will lose customers to the competition and lose even more revenue.

The way out of this dilemma is to match depreciation with obsolescence. But that is hard to do, and any speed-up in capital recovery causes a jump in telephone rates. Of course, some time later in the future, rates are lower because of this jump—but consumers and regulators focus on the rates today—not the rates five or ten years from now.

Regulators have begun to respond to the need to adjust depreciation rules to the current competitive environment, but they are moving slowly. For example, the FCC has authorized an increase in depreciation rates for telephone companies. The new rates do not yet fully reflect the impact of the new technology.

For example, in a recent case the FCC allowed several telephone companies to increase the rate of their depreciation. That increase was only equivalent to using an average lifetime of 14 years instead of 18 years to recover the costs of a telephone plant. Fourteen years is a long time in a high technology industry like telecommunications. On the other hand, the vast investment in a telephone plant means that this slight increase in depreciation rates had a short-term effect of adding another $1 billion a year to consumers' telephone bills.

Current depreciation practices tie the hands of AT&T and the operating companies. Their ability to update and modernize networks is significantly limited by the decisions state and federal regulators make on depreciation policy. Depreciation policy may lock the telephone industry into obsolete hardware and may turn outmoded technology into a dragging anchor holding back the spun-off operating companies' and AT&T's long-distance service in their competitive battles. Yet, speeding up depreciation rates is a difficult political decision since faster depreciation—no matter how socially desirable in the long run—translates directly into immediately higher telephone bills.

CONCLUSION

Changing technology was a key part of the move toward a competitive communications industry in the United States. New technology made competition easier and created the need for new kinds of communications services. Unfortunately, adopting newer technologies is unnecessarily difficult for the divested operating companies because of overly restrictive depreciation policies—policies which were designed to fit a monopoly industry and slowly changing technology.

Depreciation policy illustrates well the difficulties of transition in the communications industry. The move to more realistic depreciation rates imposes a sudden jump in telephone rates—a jump which is resisted by consumers and some regulators. It would have been easier on consumers and easier politically if realistic depreciation policies had been phased in over the last ten years. The transition would have been smoother.

Similarly, the transition at Bell Labs may have been unavoidable—but it could have been much smoother. Bell Labs will probably survive the transition and will remain one of the world's best industrial research laboratories. But, the rapid restructuring—the quick transition—poses an unnecessary threat to a unique institution. As with depreciation policy, the transition at Bell Labs could have begun earlier and proceeded more smoothly and with less cost than was actually the case.

NOTES

1. Bell Labs. 1982. *Facts About Bell Laboratories*, 12th Edition. Short Hills, New Jersey, Bell Laboratories.

2. These decisions formally occurred in the FCC's Above 890, Hush-A-Phone, Carterfone, and Domsat orders.

3. Brian W. Kernighan and Samuel P. Morgan, "The UNIX Operating System: A Model for Software Design," in *Science*, Vol. 215, 12 February 1982.

4. Floyd Kvamme (Chairman, National Semiconductor) quoted in *Revolution in Miniature, The History and Impact of Semiconductor Electronics*, Ernest Braun and Stuart MacDonald, Cambridge, Cambridge University Press, 1978, 133.

5. *Wall Street Journal*, 12 May 1983, p. 27.

6. *See*, for example, the discussion in "Chip Wars: The Japanese Threat," *Business Week*, special report, May 23, 1983, 80.

7. "Chip Wars: The Japanese Threat," *Business Week*, special report, May 23, 1983, 82.

8. This is the FCC's DTS service, also known to some as X-TEN.

6
REGULATION AND PUBLIC POLICY AFTER DIVESTITURE

The FCC and Congress

by Henry Geller

With one exception, the Modified Final Judgment (the MFJ or settlement) greatly assisted the Federal Communications Commission (FCC) in carrying out the agency's program in the common carrier telecommunications field. It cut through several long-pending FCC proceedings, and quickly produced changes necessary to introduce competition to this field. In theory, it left undiminished the Commission's authority to act under Title II of the Communications Act of 1934. Although, in practice, the FCC will find it difficult to derail the "Greene express train" and thus to take action inconsistent with the MFJ. This can have serious future consequences in an area of great disagreement between Court and agency: the restrictions on the Bell Operating Companies (BOCs) as to enhanced and information services.

Finally, the settlement wiped out all chance for comprehensive legislation, especially dealing with AT&T's structure and manner of participation in the new competitive milieu. Indeed, prospects for needed and more narrow legislation remain in doubt.

IMPACT ON THE FCC'S PROGRAM AND KEY DECISIONS

The Commission's initial aims in its competitive thrust in this field were modest. The end result was much more drastic, because the Commission found itself on the proverbial "slippery slope." Thus, the Commission began the process with its 1959 decision allowing parties to build their own private microwave systems;[1] moved to permitting a new carrier, MCI, to provide private line microwave service in 1968;[2] generally allowed such service to other specialized carriers in 1971;[3] and authorized domestic fixed satellite common carriers in 1972.[4]

The Commission believed, in making these decisions, that it had opened only the private line service, rather than the switched message toll service (MTS) so critical to the subsidy system that had been established to facilitate universal service at reasonable rates. It took court decisions in the *Execunet* cases[5] to establish that whatever the Commission's intentions, its grants were unconditional, and therefore could be used for *any* service.

A similar progression occurred as to customer premises equipment (CPE)—from *Hush-a-Phone* in 1956 when the Commission permitted AT&T to refuse interconnection and was reversed by the court,[6] to *Carterfone* in 1959[7] when the Commission ordered interconnection for specialized equipment, to the final round in the mid-1970s when interconnection for all equipment meeting specified technical standards was required.[8]

But, while the agency could be faulted for its shortsighted vision over this period, by the time of the MFJ it had come to the end of the slippery slope, and its policies were clear:

- The common carrier telecommunications area is driven by fast-changing technology, requiring a corresponding fast response in the marketplace rather than a slow-moving administrative minuet. Economic regulation, with its need to seek entry permission and its tariff restrictions (rate of return), must be avoided, wherever feasible.
- Further, this trend is accentuated by the growing merger of data communications and data processing. Both are based upon the computer—the integrated circuit. Equipment can be used for data processing and data communications, and should be so used. Enhanced services—transmission with value-added data processing such as storage, editing, code conversion, and interfacing of different machines—are rapidly coming on stream. Because data processing is unregulated and data/voice communication is regulated, the agency was forced to choose. Wisely, it opted for deregulation—the fast response in the marketplace.

By January of 1982, these broad policies had been translated into the following specifics:

- There is open entry for all CPE meeting minimum electrical standards for protection of the network. The telephone line is now like the power line. Further, all CPE offered by carriers is deregulated (new CPE on January 1, 1983, with so-called "embedded" or existing CPE to follow).[9]
- Similarly, enhanced services have been deregulated. The attempt in the *Computer Inquiry I*[10] to regulate those services predominantly communications, as opposed to those predominantly data processing, has ended. The

1980 *Computer Inquiry II* decision ruled that only transmission is regulated.

- In transmission, open entry in all interexchange markets is in the public interest.[11] Further, the Commission has relieved the tariff burdens on the carriers having no monopoly market power[12] and is clearly moving to deregulate—or, stated differently, to forbear from economic regulation (rate of return)[13] in such circumstances.
- Most important, the FCC's long-range goal in this transition is clear: to move the *entire* industry to full, effective competition and thus to full deregulation. The Commission has recognized that its effort to protect the public interest through rate regulation has been a failure in the competitive milieu,[14] and that only full, effective competition would do the trick.

If this were the airline or trucking industry, the agency would have opted for industry-wide deregulation on a fairly shortened time schedule. But the presence of a very dominant carrier, AT&T, greatly complicates the deregulatory task in this field in several respects.

CPE/Enhanced Services

While AT&T must be allowed to offer CPE and enhanced services on a deregulated basis, it has a huge *de facto* monopoly base (MTS/WATS). There is, therefore, a possibility of unfair competition. If there are joint and common costs between the monopoly and competitive sides, AT&T may pass more of those costs onto the monopoly ratepayer than is warranted, thus unfairly burdening that ratepayer and handicapping competitors.

To prevent this improper cross-subsidization, the Commission required in *Computer Inquiry II* that AT&T use for its deregulated, competitive enterprises a fully separated subsidiary (FSS), which would not have any facilities in common with the parent and which would take transmission facilities from the parent under a tariff or contract and thus would make such facilities available to others on the same terms.

There was an additional serious problem. Under the 1956 consent decree ending the 1949 government suit,[15] AT&T was restricted to common carrier communications services, the rates for which are subject to tariff regulation. The purpose was to ensure that governmental regulation would protect the public interest against this huge monopoly.

But the restriction clearly posed a large obstacle to the FCC's new program—to deregulate CPE and enhanced services, including those offered by AT&T. In *Computer Inquiry II*, the Commission construed the 1956 decree as not preventing such deregulation—on the ground that enhanced services and CPE remained ancillary activities subject to the Commission's remedial jurisdiction, and therefore the essential goal of the decree—governmental protection of the public interest—was met.

The Department of Justice (DOJ) strongly objected to this construction, and while the district court in New Jersey agreed with the FCC's construction,[16] the matter was pending on appeal to the Third Circuit and was a substantial issue in the appeals of *Computer Inquiry II* to the Court of Appeals for the District of Columbia Circuit.

MTS/WATS. The Commission could not deregulate MTS/WATS service by AT&T and its partners because of their very dominant position, over 95% of all revenues, in interstate toll service.

Interconnection. The new competitors of AT&T (called OCCs or other common carriers) had to rely on AT&T for the essential local distribution "tails." Thus, when MCI's microwave system reached Chicago, it had to interconnect with a Bell System operating company, Illinois Bell, for the "final mile" into the Chicago home or business.

But the OCCs encountered considerable difficulties in this critical interconnection process—initial refusals, delays, and a different quality of service (e.g., the need to dial many more digits, poorer technical quality, no answer supervision to indicate completion of call). The Commission had under way a proceeding to deal with these issues, but was making slow progress.[17]

Access Charges. In the monopoly situation, a complex system of industry payments, called separations and settlements, had evolved. The partners pooled their costs and revenues in the interstate (toll) area, and there was then a settlement (reimbursement of costs plus the interstate rate of return).

The separations process divided the costs between interstate and intrastate services, but did so on an arcane and arbitrary basis, designed to reduce the costs of local service and thus promote universal service at reasonable rates. This "subsidy" from interstate to intrastate was considerable, and resulted in the large interstate user paying far more than its costs, because the non-traffic-sensitive costs of access were being recovered through usage-sensitive prices.

In a competitive milieu, however, difficult problems arose. AT&T and its partners wanted the OCCs to pay their share of the subsidy. But the OCCs balked. The parties agreed to a compromise, whereby for a set period of years the OCCs would pay up to 55 percent of the subsidy element.[18]

Even more serious, with competition the system had to stop overcharging the large toll users since they now had alternatives, such as satellite or private microwave systems, and would increasingly use these alternatives. In short, competition was forcing the system to cease giving false economic signals, and to move to rational costing methods. The Commission again had instituted proceedings to deal with the new situation, but the proposals were flawed and progress was slow.[19]

BOC Procurement

The Bell System's vertical integration, resulting in over 80% BOC purchase of Western Electric equipment, also posed a difficult issue for the agency. Indeed, the Commission had been struggling with the issues of opening up BOC procurement for years—with no effective implementation in sight.[20]

The general effect of the MFJ was to greatly assist the Commission in all the above areas.

Deregulation of CPE and Enhanced Services

As stated, the FCC was greatly concerned over its interpretation of the 1956 Consent Decree, allowing AT&T to engage in CPE and enhanced services on a non-tariff basis. AT&T's main purpose in entering into the settlement was elimination of the decree, permitting its full entry into the information/enhanced services.[21] The MFJ thus mooted this difficult legal issue, and pulled the rug out from all the *Computer Inquiry II* petitioners in this critical respect.

The MFJ has led to problems in meshing its provisions with *Computer Inquiry II*—for example, as to embedded CPE. Under the MFJ, all embedded CPE goes to AT&T, which has petitioned the FCC to detariff embedded CPE *before* divestiture so that the fully separated subsidiary (FSS) can also handle this equipment. But problems like this are transitory. Indeed, there is a larger transitional problem—namely, the difficulty of administering the line between "basic" (transmission) and "enhanced"—a process that appears to signal a great deal more regulation than had been contemplated in *Computer Inquiry II*.[22] The definition is sound from an engineering point of view, but may not be wholly sound from a policy or practical viewpoint.

Note, however, that this latter difficulty in no way stems from the MFJ. The theory of the MFJ is that the interstate area is now contestable, or in the DOJ's words, "workably competitive," and that in any event, the FSS concept adds little to effective competition, since it does not at all affect the *incentive* to anti-competitive behavior.[23]

The implementation difficulties of *Computer Inquiry II* thus stem from the Commission's own view that cross-subsidization remains a serious problem because AT&T still possesses monopoly power, and that the FSS is an effective and worthwhile stratagem to deal with this problem. The MFJ indicates that the Commission is heading in the right direction—full, effective competition in the interstate arena and thus full deregulation, with no need for the FSS or the distinction between "enhanced" and "basic" services.

Interconnection.   First, by divestiture, the MFJ removed any incentive of the BOCs to discriminate against the OCCs. It also prescribed that access to the local exchange network shall be "equal in type, quality, and price to that provided AT&T. . . ." And it set forth deadlines for phasing in the equal access, with specific guidelines: the BOCs must begin to offer such access by 1984, carriers must be able to obtain equal access for one-third of their subscribers by 1985, and such access must be furnished to all subscribers "upon *bona fide* request" by 1986. Further, the MFJ dealt in considerable detail with other facets of equal interconnection (e.g., number of digits to be dialed for long-distance calls, billing, etc.).

The settlement thus cut through the indecision of the Commission in handling this critical problem. The Commission can still go forward and, as it noted,[24] impose "additional or accelerated interconnection requirements" pursuant to the Communications Act (Section 201[a], 47 U.S.C. 201[a]). It also is dealing with the similar interconnection issues as to the independent telephone companies. But the essential policy and thrust of interconnection are set by the MFJ, and the Commission will undoubtedly build on that detailed foundation.[25]

Access.   The settlements process for compensation for the origination and termination of interexchange services offered by AT&T and its partners raised serious questions of undue preference. The Commission had therefore concluded that discrimination among interexchange carriers could best be remedied by establishing a system of access charges to compensate exchange carriers for the origination and termination of interstate toll services. The MFJ tied in well: as the Commission noted in a filing with the court, "an exchange-interexchange separation that corresponds with the access charge system would facilitate the implementation of the Commission's present plans."

Further, with its requirement that the BOC provide exchange access and services "on an unbundled tariff basis . . ." and that the charge for each tariffed service must be "cost justified" on an element by element basis, the MFJ markedly affected the FCC's access proposals. It led the Commission to move away, to a very substantial extent, from the notion of uniform, nationwide access charges and instead propose access charges that would be based largely on tariffs—not on intra- and inter-corporate transfer payments—and that would end the AT&T-supervised transfer mechanism and national pooling.[26]

In its December 1982 decision, the Commission acted along these lines.[27] It particularly sought to rationalize the pricing of the non-traffic-sensitive (NTS) plants.[28]

Significantly, the MFJ does not rule out any subsidy system that the FCC and the states decide to impose.[29] The approach adopted by the FCC is much more cost-based, in part because of the new competitive environment brought on by the MFJ (e.g., the BOCs are on their own and are more vulnerable), and thus the need to phase out false economic signals leading to bypass.

This is not to say that the access scheme adopted by the Commission represents perfection. It remains flawed. The non-traffic-sensitive costs are still being recovered to a significant extent on a usage basis—an inappropriate action. There is still to be a subsidy factor, now administered by the Commission, and thus to some extent still a false economic signal. Further, the subsidy is not well targeted: it goes to high cost areas and thus could include ski resorts and summer vacation homes, instead of being directed strictly at those persons in need of assistance in order to remain on the network. But the Commission's action is clearly a step in the right direction and an improvement over the present situation. And, as stated, the MFJ provided substantial impetus.

BOC Procurement

Both the Commission and Congress had been struggling with the issues of opening up BOC procurement. Legislation in the 97th Congress (S. 898, H.R. 5158) dealt with the issue but in a way that had many disadvantages (i.e., requiring gradually increasing procurement from non-Western Electric sources for a 10-year period and up to 20 percent). The MFJ largely solved the problem by divestiture. It removed any incentive for the BOCs to favor Western Electric on the basis of affiliation. And while problems may remain, the essential thrust of policy has again been set by the MFJ.

Most important, the drastically changed structure under the MFJ facilitates competition and thus brings the FCC much closer to its goal—full competition, full deregulation.

IMPACT OF MFJ ON FCC'S AUTHORITY:
AREAS OF CONFLICT

Structural Aspects

The main thrust of the MFJ is not behavioral. The divestiture of the BOCs, the bottleneck local distribution "tails," is *structural*. The Commission found that "the basic settlement appears to be fair and reasonable" and seems to promote the overall industry plan that had evolved. In any event, the Commission conceded that it only had limited authority concerning the structure of the telephone industry. Thus, structural change of the drastic nature involved in the MFJ is largely left to the antitrust court, and does not interfere with any limited authority of the agency.

Non-structural Aspects

In its *amicus* brief to the district court, the FCC made clear its great interest in the non-structural aspects of the settlement (effect on industry, rates, interconnection, access, etc.) and its responsibilities under the Communications Act to pass on the applications that must be filed to implement the MFJ. It noted the possibility of conflicts in several areas: the requirement for divestiture within 18 months, if the Commission could not make its public interest finding (Section 214) under the Act within that same time period; adoption by the Commission of access rate elements, computation methods, etc., that might differ from the MFJ requirements; and possible interconnection differences.

The Commission argued (Amicus Br. 48) that the antitrust court should not enter any decree ". . . in such a way as 1) to circumscribe future actions a regulatory agency has the authority to take, or 2) to defeat an essential purpose embodied in a regulatory statute." And it requested the following specific language:[30]

> Nothing in this decree shall be construed to affect any power conferred by law upon the Federal Communications Commission.

In its opinion of August 11, 1982, the District Court rejected the addition of the clause, stating that it "would have no effect either on the authority of the Commission or that of the Court. . . ." Noting that the FCC found the basic settlement to be "fair and reasonable," with "no difficulties with regard to implementation," the Court stated that it would not anticipate conflict. But if it occurred, the Court held, "the judgment of antitrust court should prevail" in view of the FCC's "limited authority in regard to structural matters."

The divestiture plan does require prior FCC authority for transfer of facilities (Sections 214, 221, 310[d]) or discontinuance of service (Section 214).[31] The FCC and the antitrust court are thus both "sovereign," in contrast to state law or regulation which must give way. It is clear, therefore, that the two must work together.

It would also appear that as a practical matter, the District Court will generally prevail. It is on a faster track, and any derailment or slowdown has the most serious consequences for AT&T (and thus for the settlement). Whatever the legal theory may be, the practicalities are that the District Court had the whiphand until divestiture was effected in early 1984.[32]

This is not to say that the District Court can roam at will and invade the agency's turf. The Court thus rejected arguments that it should deal with the present level of BOC charges to the OCCs (the "ENFIA" controversy); it noted that this matter has been dealt with by the FCC, and is under active review by the agency and the courts.[33] Similarly, while the District Court used net book to value assets for the purposes of the MFJ, that decision "in no way affects the authority of regulators to use a different standard in valuing assets within their jurisdiction for ratemaking purposes."

The Conflict Over Access Charges

In its April 20, 1983 opinion on the LATA issue (local access transport areas), the District Court strongly disagreed with the Commission's approach as to access charges. First, it observed that there was no conclusive evidence that long-distance revenues have been subsidizing local rates, and second, even assuming that they were, the subsidy could continue through access charges placed on the carriers.

The Court was distressed that the Commission had sought to make up for the lost "subsidy" by charges placed primarily on residential subscribers. It acknowledged that "the FCC is not bound by the Court's decisions or assumptions in regard to access charges" but noted that "the availability of the access charge in the form used by the Commission is directly tied to the decree. . . ."

It is difficult to follow the Court's reasoning. The driving force here is the new competitive milieu, with its threat of bypass, if the old system is continued. Under that system, the cost of local loops is, on average, $26 per month per subscriber loop. While this cost is non-traffic-sensitive (i.e., it exists whether or not the phone is used), most of this access cost—including the entire $7 average per line assigned to the FCC's interstate ratemaking—is now recovered in usage sensitive rates, and consequently, from many subscribers who pay too little and a very few who pay their costs many times over.

Thus, one percent of the BOCs' subscribers account for 42 percent of the revenue necessary to recover the $7 per line per month (interstate average) for all subscribers. The average access payment of these high volume customers is about $160 per line—23 times the price they would be charged on a NTS basis for their NTS plant.[34]

These customers will not continue to pay $60 to a BOC for interstate access to the interexchange network if there is an alternative. There are bypass alternatives today, in the form of coaxial cable, fiber, link microwave, satellite, digital termination service, and cellular radio. The District Court's rather casual observation that bypass is not an "imminent threat" is simply wrong.

Bypass is feasible today and will grow, particularly if false economic signals are given.[35] The BOCs are vulnerable, because their rate structures focus the incentives for bypass in a relatively few easy-to-find large users. Nor is there any help in the Court's point to place the charge on the carriers; such a charge would simply be passed through to the toll customer.

It is therefore critical that steps be taken *now* to gradually rationalize the system so that any bypass is economically justified, and not induced by the continuation of inappropriate rate structures.

The District Court continues to show great concern over the FCC's access action. While acknowledging that it lacks authority to countermand this decision, it took it into account in passing upon trade name, trademark, and patent issues. In all these instances, its decision to favor the BOCs "was buttressed by the need to cope with the threat posed to universal, low-cost, local telephone service."[36]

Treatment of BOCs: The Most Important Area of Conflict

The District Court stated that it did not anticipate any conflict with the FCC, but at that very time it was presented with an important and very large conflict: the restrictions on BOC activity.

Justice's theory of the case is that with the MFJ it has separated the "workably competitive" (toll, CPE, enhanced services) from the natural monopoly (local exchange). The MFJ thus confines the BOCs to telecommunications exchange or access services (or a "natural monopoly service actually regulated by tariff").

Under this view, if the BOCs could engage in manufacture and sale of CPE, enhanced services of interexchange activities, they would favor their own operations through control of the essential local facilities, and could improperly cross-subsidize from the local exchange monopoly base.

In its submission to the Court, the FCC strongly disagreed (Amicus Br., 29–52). It argued that the anticompetitive problems in the suit stemmed from AT&T's actions; the seven new operating companies are different entities, differently placed. Their competition in the telecommunications field (competing with AT&T in particular) is needed. Cross-subsidization with the local monopoly case is not feasible practically, and in any event, regulation can deal with this unlikely occurrence. Further, interconnection is specified, and the BOC transmission facilities must be available, on the same terms and conditions, to all other information/enhanced service providers. Under the circumstances, the FCC urged, the BOC restrictions should be lifted now, or alternatively, should expire in five years.

The District Court largely rejected the Commission's arguments as inconsistent with the basic concept of the settlement. The Court did require the modification allowing the BOCs to sell (but not manufacture) equipment, and to have the printed *Yellow Pages* business. Further, it added a provision that the restrictions "shall be removed upon a showing by the petitioning BOC that there is no substantial possibility that it could use its monopoly power to impede competition in the market it seeks to enter."

It is not my purpose here to referee between the FCC and the DOJ/court position.[37] I would briefly note again that suppression of competition is a drastic remedy—a last resort. Moreover, if AT&T is motivated to dismember itself so that it can enter the new information/enhanced services, it is difficult to perceive why the BOCs—$17–21 billion telecommunications enterprises—should not be given the same opportunity, with appropriate safeguards.

Stated differently, does it serve the public interest if GTE were kept from competing in enhanced services, and if it does not, why should Pacific Telephone be treated differently than GTE?

There are two legal issues that merit consideration: 1) Could the District Court have modified the decree, as urged by the FCC?, and 2) If it refused to do so (as it did), could the FCC have prevailed upon appeal? In each case, I believe that the answer is yes.

Under the Tunney Act, the District Court could consider whether the proposed decree served the public interest.[38] This does not mean that the Court could revise the decree as it desired, or fashion one that it believed better suited the antitrust suit. A consent decree is, after all, a compromise between the parties, and as long as it is reasonably within the ballpark of the suit, the court oversteps its boundaries and invades the turf of the Executive Branch if it intervenes to impose antitrust nuances.[39]

On the other hand, the decree is one of a court of equity, and as such, the court is required to be assured that the overall public interest is being served by its entry. In that sense, the revisions of the Tunney Act, opening up the process for meaningful comment, serve a most worthwhile purpose.

If the above analysis is correct, the District Court was probably incorrect in its actions fine tuning the antitrust aspects (e.g., the *Yellow Pages*). It could, however, consider the broad policy matters raised by the FCC as they dealt with a basic issue for the equity court: does this decree serve the public interest in light of the positions and arguments expressed by the expert agency, to whom Congress has delegated the fashioning of overall communications policy?

The District Court rejected the Commission's arguments, and, again on practicality, this is probably the only course it could have taken. It was one thing to work minor changes, and another to undermine, to a large extent, DOJ's whole notion of the case and the settlement. Such a revision would quite likely be rejected by DOJ, resulting in appeal of a settlement that had to be implemented in the most expeditious fashion. Indeed, it is dubious that, in that event, the settlement would have held together.

As to what would have happened if the FCC had appealed, the case would have undoubtedly been a difficult, close one, and we are necessarily speculating on what the Supreme Court would do in a hypothetical situation. The argument of Justice that the fashioning of *structural* relief is for the District Court, which left an appropriate escape hatch with its provision for future BOC petitions, is a substantial one. In my view, however, the Commission would have had an excellent chance of prevailing: It *is* the expert agency, and its argument that DOJ is repeating the mistakes of the 1956 settlement, this time at the BOC level, and frustrating communications policy, would carry great weight.

But for the same reasons of practicality, the agency acquiesced. So the next round, which is sure to come, will be on the petition of the BOCs; if the BOC entry in the enhanced/information services is blocked by the District Court, the Commission should enter again, and this time, with no urgent time constraints, should advance its arguments, including those of primary jurisdiction in this particular area.

IMPACT ON LEGISLATION

In October of 1981, the Senate, by a 90–4 vote, passed S. 898, a comprehensive re-working of Title II of the Communications Act, that *inter alia,* would have overruled the 1956 Consent Decree and allowed AT&T to enter, on a deregulated basis but with an FSS, the new enhanced services and the CPE field. The House bill, H.R. 5158, was along the same lines, but with more restrictions placed on AT&T activities. Indeed, probably as a result of its survey of the House situation, AT&T decided that it could only obtain the goal it sought through the judicial process. It therefore made its deal with DOJ in January 1982.

The MFJ, of course, made moot S. 898, passed before its announcement and proceeding on a different premise (FSS: behavioral regulations). The House did seek to revise H.R. 5158 after the MFJ, and specified a different structure for AT&T (e.g., Long Lines would become the separated entity, instead of the CPE/enhanced service provided) and several different requirements than in the MFJ.

But AT&T had made its deal: it had agreed to spin off two-thirds of its assets (the BOCs) in order to enter the new information fields on a deregulated basis. It was in no mood to agree to further restrictions. It could block legislation,[40] and it went all out to do so. Congressman Wirth, Chairman of the House Subcommittee on Telecommunications, finally gave up the struggle, and telecommunications legislation died in the 97th Congress.

There is every indication that such comprehensive legislation is also dead in the 98th Congress. First, there is clearly no possibility of legislation dealing with the AT&T structural issue. Chairman Packwood of the Senate Commerce Committee has stated that he believes a simplified bill should be enacted, dealing with access (and particularly universal service at reasonable rates), national defense, clarification of the FCC's authority to deregulate, and extension of FCC authority over intrastate toll service.

But Congress seems unlikely to move forward, for several reasons. First, a simplified bill does not remain "simple" in light of industry pressures. Second, with one or two exceptions, the above areas now seem not to require urgent legislative attention.[41]

The one sure exception is the need to bring intrastate tolls within federal regulation. The present dichotomy makes no technical or practical sense. But while remedial legislation is clearly desirable, it faces strong resistance from the state public utilities commissions, and Congress shows little indication of "biting the bullet."

The other possible area is the access charge. As good politicians, but probably bad economists, Congress remains much concerned over rising local telephone charges. Several bills have been introduced to deal with the problem.[42] Their approach—to impose the NTS charge on carriers and those engaged in bypass—is a definite possibility for enactment, but is seriously flawed.

Congress can reasonably make the policy judgment in favor of a subsidy system to ensure universal service at reasonable rates. But the public interest would be much better served if such a scheme targeted those too poor otherwise to afford access (lifeline) telephone service. Congress shows no indication at all of a willingness to so proceed.

The failure to enact legislation certainly reflects adversely upon the Congress. Policy should be made by the Congress, not the courts.

It would be a mistake, however, to say that the legislative process did not play an important role. It did in several respects:

- AT&T had one consistent goal: to overrule the 1956 decree and be allowed to enter wholly the new information services. It sought that goal from Congress, and only when it reluctantly concluded that Congress could not act to its satisfaction, did it turn to the judicial route. In short, Congressional failure ironically was part of a mosaic that convinced AT&T that it was simply too big—that it could not achieve its purpose of unfettered entry into new competitive areas, with the enormous baggage of the BOC monopolies.
- The legislative "rewrite" process, and former Chairman Lionel Van Deerlin in particular, deserves great credit for setting the stage for *Computer Inquiry II*. The "rewrite" legislation made possible the mood allowing the agency to take such a strong step.

- The legislative effort, in both the 96th and 97th Congress, greatly influenced the antitrust case (e.g., the ban on electronic publishing by AT&T, *Yellow Pages* to BOCs, CPE sale permitted to BOCs).
- Further, oversight hearings had their effect. Thus, these hearings in both Houses delivered a clear message to the FCC to phase in cost-based access charges and to maintain a subsidy system to promote universal service at reasonable rates.

In sum, the intense legislative effort of the last five years for a comprehensive bill has crested, and will now recede in light of the MFJ and the implementation process. The future will probably involve more oversight and, at most, narrow legislation dealing with access charges and the federal-state dichotomy.

NOTES

1. Allocation of Microwave Frequencies in the Bands Above 890 Mc, 27 FCC 359 (1959), *recon. denied,* 29 FCC 825 (1960).

2. *Microwave Communications, Inc.*, 18 FCC 2d 953 (1969), *reconsideration denied,* 21 FCC 2d 190 (1970).

3. *Specialized Common Carriers,* 29 FCC 2d 870, 31 FCC 2d 1106 (1971), *aff'd. sub. nom.*, Washington Utilities and Transportation Commission v. FCC, 513 F.2d 1142 (9th Cir.), *cert. denied,* 423 U.S. 834 (1975).

4. *Domestic Communications Satellite Facilities,* 35 FCC 2d 844, 38 FCC 2d 665 (1972).

5. MCI Telecommunications Corp. v. FCC (Execunet I), 561 F.2d 365 (D.C. Cir. 1977), *cert. denied,* 434 U.S. 1040 (1978); (Execunet I), 580 F.2d 590 (D.C. Cir. 1978), *cert. denied,* 439 U.S. 980 (1978).

6. Hush-a-Phone Corp. v. U.S., 238 F2d 266 (D.C. Cir. 1956).

7. 13 FCC 2d 240, 14 FCC 2d 571 (1968).

8. *Second Report and Order,* Docket 19528, 58 FCC 2d 736 (1976); *Telephone Equipment Registration,* Docket 21182, 67 FCC 2d 1343 (1978).

9. *Computer II Final Decision,* 77 FCC 2d 384 (1980), reconsideration, 84 FCC 2d 50 (1980), *affirmed* CCIA v. FCC, 693 F.2d 198 (D.C. Cir. 1982), *cert. denied,* 103 S.C t. 2109 (1983).

10. 28FCC 2d 291 (1970), 28 FCC 2d 267 (1971), *aff'd. in part sub nom.* GTE Service Corp. v. FCC, 474 F.2d 724 (2d Cir. 1973), *decision on remand,* 40 FCC 2d 293 (1973).

11. *MTS and WATS Market Structure,* Docket 78- 72, 81 FCC 2d 177 (1980).

12. First Report and Order, 85 FCC 2d 1 (1980); Second Report and Order, 91 FCC 2d 59 (1982).

13. This action has already been taken as to the resale carrier (i.e., those using the transmission facilities of other carriers), *Second Report and Order, Policy and Rules Concerning Rates for Competitive Carrier Services*, 91 FCC 2d 59 (1982), *recon. denied*, FCC 83-96 (March 21, 1983) and will undoubtedly be shortly extended to other types of non-dominant carriers. *See Deregulation of Telecommunications Services, Further Notice of Proposed Rulemaking* in Docket No. 78-72, 84 FCC 2d 445 (1981).

14. *See*, e.g., L. Johnson, *Competition and Cross-Subsidization in the Telephone Industry*, R-2976-RC/NSF, December 1982, for a full treatment of this aspect; *see also* G. W. Brock, *The Telecommunications Industry*, Harvard Univ. Press, Cambridge, Mass., 1981, 222-23.

15. U.S. v. Western Electric Company, Inc., Civ. Action No. 17-49 (D.N.J.).

16. U.S. v. Western Electric Co., 1981-82 Trade Cases 764, 275 (D.N.J. 1981).

17. *Supplemental Notice of Inquiry and Proposed Rulemaking*, CC Docket 78-72, 73 FCC 2d 222 (1979).

18. *Exchange Network Facilities for Interstate Access (ENFIA)*, 71 FCC 2d 440 (1978); 90 FCC 2d 1, 18 (1982).

19. *Second Supplemental Notice*, 77 FCC 2d 224 (1980).

20. *See* Docket No. 19129, 1976-77 FCC pronouncements; FCC Docket CC 80-53.

21. Explaining its rationale for accepting Justice's proposed modification, counsel for AT&T stated: "The technology of telecommunications has so merged with the technology of data processing that if we end up with the 1956 Consent Decree we are a withering corporation waiting for its demise and nothing more." Mr. Saunders, transcript, U.S. v. AT&T, Case No. 74-1898 (DDC) vol. 134, P.M. Sess., January 12, 1982, p. 25027.

22. There are roughly 15 pending petitions for construction or waiver of the basic/enhanced requirements of *Computer II. See*, e.g., *In the Matter of Tymnet*, March 16, 1983 (FCC 3018).

23. Significantly however, as a condition to its approval of GTE's recent acquisition of Southern Pacific Communications (with its MTS Sprint service), DOJ insisted upon a separate subsidiary for the competitive enterprises (except for CPE). *Telecommunications Reports*, Vol. 49, No. 18, May 9, 1983, 1-6.

24. *See* FCC Amicus Curiae Brief to District Court, 26.

25. Thus, whatever the Commission might have wished to decide for interconnection, e.g., at a Class 4 office or tandem switch instead of the Class 5 (local) office interconnection under the MFJ, the practicalities are that the MFJ will control, because it is in place.

26. *MTS and WATS Market Structure* (Second Supplemental Notice), 77 FCC 2d 224 (1980); *Fourth Supplemental Notice*, 90 FCC 2d 135 (1982).

27. *See In the Matter of MTS and WATS Market Structure*, CC Docket No. 78-72, Phase I, adopted December 22, 1982, FCC 82-579, *appeal pending* MCI Telecommunications Corp. v. FCC, No. 82-1237 (D.C. Cir. filed Mar. 4, 1982).

28. This is the equipment that must be in place in order to afford access to the network, local or long-distance, i.e., the inside wiring, the line back to the first switching hub (class 5 office), and the switch dedicated to that subscriber. To pay for this equipment, under the Commission's decision, as of January 1, 1984 residential subscribers will be assessed at least $2 per line per month (and $4 per business line per month). Interexchange carriers will also pay a portion of these NTS costs but gradually the subscribers' share will rise until in 1989 they will bear a substantial percentage of the NTS costs. In addition to the flat fee, both carriers and subscribers will also pay a fee per interstate/foreign call, and a surcharge will be utilized to establish a fund for use in high cost areas, in order to promote universal service at reasonable rates.

29. Thus, the District Court in the August 11, 1982 opinion stated that "the decree leave[s] state and federal regulators with a mechanism—access charges—by which to require a subsidy *from intercity service to local service.* By means of these access charges, the regulators would be free to maintain local rates at current levels or they could so set the charges as to increase or decrease local rates (emphasis added)." [U.S. v. AT&T, 552 F.Supp. 131, 169 (D.D.C. 1982), *aff'd.,* Maryland v. U.S., 103 S.C t. 1204 (1983); *see also ibid.* 169, n. 161; 224, n. 376].

30. Memorandum of the FCC as Amicus Curiae, 62 F.C.C. 2d 1102 (December 30, 1975).

31. *See* Letter of January 13, 1983 to AT&T, requesting detailed data so that the Commission could make the public interest judgments required under Title II, Preliminary Analysis of AT&T Plan, Common Carrier Bureau, Feb., 1983, C 1-3.

32. It is for that practical reason that the District Court could "push" Justice into accepting its requirement that the BOCs be allowed to sell (but not manufacture) CPE. Justice strongly disagrees with this modification (*see* DOJ Brief in Supreme Court, Maryland v. U.S., Oct. term, 1983, Nos. 82-952, 28-29, n. 35), but as a practical matter could not appeal and thus delay the divestiture process, with all its attendant costs and instabilities for AT&T. The same practical consequences foreclose the Commission from upsetting the decree at this time by taking appeals or withholding certification.

33. *See Exchange Network Facilities (ENFIA),* 90 FCC 2d 1 (1982), *affirmed,* MCI Telecommunications Corp. v. FCC, No. 82-1553 (D.C. Cir., June 24, 1983).

34. *See FCC En Banc Hearing,* Docket 78-72, November 29, 1982, Tr. 219-20; BOC Docket 78-72 Comments at 11-12, 46-47, 92.

35. *See* FCC Response to Common Carrier Questions of Chairman Dingell, Appendix, Status Report on Near-Term Local Bypass Developments (1983); *The Office,* March 1981, 106-110; *Satellite News,* March 22, 1982, 3; *Computerworld,* March 21, 1982, 1.

36. Opinion of District Court, Civ. Act. 82-0192, July 8, 1983, 76; *see also* 154.

37. AT&T at all times stated that it did not oppose the removal of BOC restrictions; that this was a matter for DOJ, which had insisted upon them. The author, together with the editors of this book, filed comments with the District Court, urging the inappropriateness of the BOC restrictions, and in particular those preventing the BOC from rendering information/enhanced services. *See* Comments of Henry Geller, Harry M. Shooshan III, Charles Jackson, Ira Barron and Catherine M. Reiss, in Civ. Action No. 74-1698, April 14, 1982.

38. *See* cases cited, 552 F.Supp. at 147–153. The Tunney Act essentially changed process but not substantive law.

39. If the Antitrust Division dismissed a complaint on the ground that it believed its limited resources could be better used in several other areas, it is difficult to see how that action, peculiarly within the discretion of the Executive Branch, is subject to review by the Article III court. But the same considerations can enter into a consent decree settlement, and thus, unless patently not within the confines of the complaint or raising broad equity issues, the settlement poses difficult problems for judicial intervention and activism, as the three dissenters to the Supreme Court's affirmance of the district court noted. *See* Maryland v. U.S., *supra.* I believe that the same time bind that so influenced all parties below was at work in the Supreme Court, and that the issues raised in the dissenting opinion are therefore likely to be considered in some future, less urgent context.

40. Several industry groups could block—but not pass—legislation in this field. It was because of this phenomenon that Congress kept accommodating groups like cable TV, the newspapers, and burglar alarm associations, with special restrictions on AT&T.

41. Process to insure that national defense factors are appropriately considered in the telecommunications policy field is now under way. Executive Order 12382, September 12, 1982, establishing the President's National Security Telecommunications Advisory Committee. As to the FCC's authority to forbear from economic regulation, the D.C. Circuit affirmed such forbearance in the special circumstances of *Computer Inquiry II*, CCIA v. FCC, *supra*, 693 F.2d, 210–212. While not conclusive, this certainly augurs well for the proposition. However, clarifying legislation would be desirable.

42. E.g., *Telecommunications Report*, June 27, 1983, 7–9.

7
REGULATION AND PUBLIC POLICY AFTER DIVESTITURE

The State Regulators

by Charles A. Zielinski

In 1969, Louis Kohlmeier, Jr. published *The Regulators*, a general condemnation of government regulation of most industries. His central argument was that government agencies had attempted to protect the industries they regulated "by minimizing the number of competitors . . . by condemning price competition among a few competitors and by restraining industrial change in the form of technological innovation." But he conceded that "government regulation of an industry can be reasonably successful when the industry involved has a true monopoly. . . ." He singled out federal and state regulation of the "national monopoly" in the telephone industry to support the latter point.[1]

Early in 1984, the "national monopoly" in the domestic telephone industry ceased to exist. The American Telephone & Telegraph Company (AT&T), the dominant company in the industry for more than a century, has divested approximately two-thirds of its assets—principally local exchange distribution and switching facilities—pursuant to the Modified Final Judgment (MFJ) that settled the government's antitrust suit against AT&T. These divested assets will be owned by separate Bell Operating Companies (BOCs) organized as seven distinct regional holding companies. The BOCs will not be allowed to transmit most phone calls between states and significant population centers. Rather, they will "deliver" calls to other companies and to consumers.

Once completed, the divestiture process will have required enormous amounts of analysis, argument, comment, and fine-tuning concerning the transfer of assets, as well as various restrictions on AT&T and the divested BOCs. In the end, however, the most fundamental change is that we will no longer be able to call upon the resources of one company to provide telephone service from our homes and businesses to the rest of the country. In this sense, the MFJ will make the telephone industry more akin to the transportation industry, where no single company offers door-to-door service from a home or business to the rest of the country.

In heavily populated urban areas, consumers generally have a variety of transportation choices. For local transportation they can usually choose among automobiles, cabs, buses and subways, for example, to go to and from their place of employment. These same methods of transportation are generally employed as the first part of a longer trip. We use local transportation to reach an airport, train or bus station, from which point we are taken to another city within our state or in another state. From the airport, bus or train terminal in that city, we again employ local transportation to reach our destination in that city.

Traveling long distances from rural areas is often less convenient and more expensive. In order to reach a distant major urban area, a rural resident may have to make a relatively long trip to the nearest major airport from which an airline provides service to the distant major city. From the airport, it will cost the rural resident no more than the urban resident to reach his or her destination, but the rural resident will have paid more to reach the airport via a bus or, perhaps, a commuter airline, assuming there is one serving the general area of his or her residence.

Urban residents traveling to rural areas, of course, face these same problems in reverse order, and a rural resident traveling to another rural area will have limited local transportation choices at the beginning and at the end of the trip.

As a result of the AT&T breakup, carriage of a telephonic communication from one point to another, like the transportation of people from one place to another, now requires the services of several companies. The analogy to the transportation industry, however, will be far from perfect, at least in the short run.

First, the BOCs—like a bus company—will now provide "local transportation" service. To complete a phone call to a destination within a specified geographic area, called "Local Access and Transport Area" (LATA), a consumer uses only the service provided by a BOC serving that area.[2] Unlike the situation in the transportation industry, however, the consumer is not likely, in the short run, to have any alternative to the BOC for "local transportation" service, either in urban or in rural areas. Moreover, the LATA in which consumer choice is limited to the BOC may be quite large, in some cases encompassing an entire state.

Second, there may be important differences in long-distance intrastate telephone service between LATAs, and service between LATAs in different states. To make an interstate long-distance call, a consumer will generally use the local transportation service of a BOC to reach the facilities of AT&T or one of its long-distance service competitors (OCCs). The call will then be transmitted over the facilities of AT&T or one of the OCCs to a point in another LATA. From that point, the call will be carried by the BOC serving that LATA to its ultimate destination. For long-distance calls between points in the same state, however, AT&T may, in some instances, be the only "inter-LATA" carrier, at least in the short run.

Finally, unlike transportation service, consumers will generally be able to purchase "door-to-door" service for long-distance calls from one carrier under a uniform pricing schedule. Although the facilities of several carriers will be used to complete long-distance calls, consumers will be able to purchase an entire "trip" from AT&T or the OCCs. The price of the trip will include "local transportation costs" paid by AT&T and the OCCs to the BOCs. Calls involving similar distances that are placed through AT&T will generally have the same regulated price. But this may not be true for the OCCs, because they have more freedom to change prices.

The extent to which price and carrier choice in the telephone industry ultimately resemble those in the transportation industry will depend largely on future government regulatory policy. The price of telephone service, as well as the carriers involved, are subject to federal and state regulation. At the federal level, the key regulatory agency is the Federal Communications Commission (FCC). At the state level, the important agency is the state public utility commission (PUC). The FCC exercises authority over all carriers that provide service between states, as well as the rates for interstate services. The PUCs govern all carriers that provide service within their respective states as well as the rates for intrastate services. Although the FCC has encouraged the development of competition for interstate services in recent years, most PUCs have accepted regulated monopoly as the instrument for providing intrastate services.

While this chapter explores the role of the PUCs after the AT&T divestiture, it cannot be covered adequately without reference to federal policy, because federal policy significantly constrains the activities of PUCs. We will therefore cover some key FCC controls on the PUCs. Next, given these limitations, we will discuss potential effects of PUC regulatory initiatives on the future provision of telephone service. Finally, we will offer some conclusions concerning the role of the PUCs.

FEDERAL POLICY AND THE PUCs

The prices charged by companies providing telephone service within a state are regulated on a "cost of service" basis. In other words, the company's expenses and its investment in facilities are the basis for its prices. Rates are designed to recover normal expenses and to produce a reasonable profit or return on investment.

Through its power to "disallow" certain types or levels of telephone company expenses and investment, a PUC can exercise control over overall price levels. Through its authority to allocate to different services the costs it does allow, and to determine whether those costs should be recovered from fixed or variable charges, a PUC can also determine the relationship between the price for simply being connected to the telephone network, for example, and the prices for making local and "toll" calls within a state.

Thus, a PUC can significantly influence what consumers pay for telephone services.[3] A PUC also derives control through its authority to grant licenses or certificates for telephone service. Through its power to deny certificates, a PUC can limit the number of competing companies that provide telephone service.

For the most part, the MFJ indirectly limits the exercise of PUC powers. In approving the MFJ, Judge Greene specifically noted that "nothing in the proposed decree would require a state to replace its regulatory system with a system of competition."[4] More specifically, the MFJ precludes a PUC from awarding a monopoly for inter-LATA service within a state to a BOC, because the MFJ generally prohibits the BOCs from providing inter-LATA service.

But a BOC could be awarded a monopoly for calls to and from points in the same LATA. Moreover, the MFJ does not prevent a PUC from granting an inter-LATA monopoly to any company other than a BOC, including AT&T.

Similarly, the MFJ requires the BOCs to *offer* "equal access" at "nondiscriminatory" rates. But, it does not prohibit PUCs from directing BOCs to provide access to only one intrastate inter-LATA carrier. Thus, the MFJ leaves a PUC with considerable regulatory discretion over telephone service between points within a state.

The FCC can limit the discretion of PUCs to a far more significant degree than Judge Greene's MFJ. In a series of court victories turning back appeals of a number of its decisions, the FCC firmly established its authority to regulate telephone facilities located within a single state, as well as the companies who own and operate those facilities, when those facilities are "links" in telephone communications between states. Thus, when the "local transportation" or intra-LATA facilities of a BOC are links in carrying a call to an inter-LATA carrier, or in delivering that call to a telephone subscriber in another state, the FCC can regulate the price for the entire "trip."

In doing so, the FCC determines what part of a BOC's total "local transportation" or intra-LATA costs (expenses plus return on investment) will be included in the cost of—and, therefore, be covered by the price of—the interstate "trips." The remaining BOC "local transportation" costs must be covered by prices for BOC intrastate telephone services that are regulated by the PUCs.

The FCC can also decide how many companies can be involved in providing interstate "trips." PUCs cannot deny access to or use of "local transportation" facilities necessary to complete "trips" between states to companies the FCC has authorized for interstate service.

A number of the judicial decisions which established this broad FCC authority involved appeals by the PUCs. Although these appeals, on their surface, seemed to be no more than arguments between federal and state regulatory agencies over interpretation of the law, they signified a fundamental difference of opinion between the FCC and most PUCs over proper regulatory policy for the telephone industry.

Around 1970, the FCC began to experiment seriously with competition in the telephone industry by authorizing OCCs to compete for AT&T's interstate private line services. These services mainly satisfied large internal business communications needs of corporations with offices located in different states. By the end of the 1970s, however, AT&T was facing competition not only in this limited business communications market, but also in its enormous market for nationwide long-distance service to all residential and business customers. AT&T also faced significant competition in the residential and business telephone equipment product market, where it had enjoyed a monopoly for many decades.

Throughout the 1970s, many PUCs, favoring continuation of a policy of regulated monopoly, unsuccessfully battled against the swing to competition fostered by the FCC. They adopted state regulations inconsistent with competition that were preempted by the FCC. They appealed the FCC preemption decisions to the courts, but their appeals were denied. The FCC maintained its overall control of policy and established its view that the public would be served better by competing companies providing a choice of telephone equipment and interstate long-distance services.

Although the PUCs were criticized for being "pro-monopoly" in these efforts—as, of course, they were—it would not be fair to dismiss their cause as mere government protection of a monopolist from competition. The PUCs implicitly recognized that monopoly was a necessary precondition to the exercise of effective government control over the prices of all telephone services. With a monopoly, the government could, for example, direct AT&T to keep its prices for telephone equipment and interstate long-distance services high and its rates for local telephone services low. As long as the *total* revenues produced by rates for *all* AT&T services covered AT&T *total* costs, there was no need for the price of each service to cover the cost of each service. Competition for high priced services, the PUCs reasoned, would ultimately force the government to allow the price of each telephone service to cover its individual costs.

The PUCs opposed this loss of government control on egalitarian grounds. They argued that the government should have the power to hold the price for subscription or "access" to the telephone network below its cost so that poor people could afford access. They suggested that other telephone services were "discretionary" or "luxury" items, the use of which should provide the revenues necessary to keep the price of access low enough to assure "universal" access to the telephone network.

In a sense, the MFJ has brought this fundamental policy conflict between the PUCs and the FCC to its inevitable conclusion. The MFJ required the FCC to develop a policy to govern the "access" charges that AT&T and the OCCs will pay the divested BOCs for delivering interstate inter-LATA calls to them, and for carrying those calls to their ultimate destination. The FCC has decided that AT&T and the OCCs should pay what amounts to gradually diminishing rates for the BOCs' "local transportation" service. Eventually, these rates will produce revenues that cover little more than the costs incurred by providing this service. In turn, subscribers will gradually assume more of the costs caused by their demand for access to the telephone network.[5]

In reaching this decision, the FCC recognized that competition will not permit regulated prices for interstate services to AT&T and the OCCs that are far above the cost of providing those services. If AT&T and the OCCs are required to pay far more than the cost of using BOC facilities, they will "bypass" the BOCs by developing their own "local transportation" facilities. To compete against bypass facilities, the BOCs would ultimately have to bring their prices for service closer to their cost of service.

Because AT&T and the OCCs will be permitted to pay prices closer to the costs BOCs incur, subscribers will have to pay prices closer to the costs of providing access to the network. At least in the short run, the shift in cost responsibility from AT&T and the OCCs to subscribers will lead to price increases for subscriber access to the telephone network. In other words, subscribers will pay higher rates without regard to the number of calls they place. At the same time, prices for long-distance calls between states should decline because "local transportation" costs for these calls will also decline.

The PUCs, for the most part, have vigorously opposed this FCC decision, which has fulfilled their prediction of the rate changes that would result from competition. They argue that prices to consumers for "access" to the network will increase, making subscription less affordable and threatening "universal access." Rates for "discretionary" long-distance services will decline.

The PUCs have taken their case to the courts and are supporting Congressional efforts to reverse the FCC's decision. If they are unsuccessful, they may try to achieve their goals by maintaining monopoly preserves and tight control of price relationships within their states.

PUC REGULATION OF INTRASTATE
TELEPHONE SERVICES

Most of the BOC costs that fall under the jurisdiction of the PUCs are recovered from rates for local service and intrastate "toll" service. In most areas of the country, local service is available at a "flat" rate. Within a defined geographic area, subscribers can make calls, to each other, of unlimited number and duration for an unvarying monthly price. Calls from the defined local calling area to other parts of the state are "toll" calls. There is an additional charge for each call and for each minute or other specified increment of time the call lasts.

Although the BOCs can no longer provide "toll" service between LATAs, some revenues formerly produced by intrastate toll rates can now come from BOC access charges to inter-LATA carriers. Thus, the PUCs, like the FCC, must devise a carrier access charge policy. With the price for subscriber access to the telephone network increasing as a result of the FCC's policy, the PUCs may attempt to establish high access rates to inter-LATA carriers for their intrastate traffic. The PUCs may believe that these high carrier access rates would produce enough revenues to permit BOCs to continue to keep subscriber access rates low and protect "universal access."

To achieve this result, some PUCs may try to preserve a monopoly for intrastate inter-LATA service. AT&T, for example, might be awarded a monopoly in return for which it would have to pay high access charges. But, this PUC action would still leave competing carriers free to offer interstate inter-LATA service to customers within the state. Customers connected to a competing inter-LATA carrier would have the capability to complete intrastate inter-LATA calls via that carrier.

Thus, to enforce its monopoly policy, the PUC might have to order its BOC to block those intrastate calls. If the BOC then had difficulty in distinguishing between interstate and intrastate calls and erroneously blocked some of the former, the FCC could regard the PUC order as leading to improper interference with interstate commerce. This, in turn, could lead to FCC preemption of the PUC order to the BOCs and might leave the PUC without the means necessary to enforce its policy.

A PUC might also permit inter-LATA intrastate competition and attempt to produce a high level of revenue from high BOC access charges to *all* competing carriers. To prevent competing inter-LATA competitors from avoiding these charges, the PUC might prohibit the use of alternative "local transportation" or "bypass" facilities for intrastate calls.

To enforce its prohibition, the PUC might have to order blocking of intrastate calls via bypass facilities. BOCs may have difficulty distinguishing between interstate and intrastate calls delivered via "bypass" facilities. Blocking of interstate calls could lead to preemption of the PUC's directive by the FCC.

"Bypass" facilities may, of course, take a variety of forms. One possible form is a cable television system with switching capability, which some new cable systems already have. A switched cable television system, capable of carrying voice signals, would amount to almost complete duplication of the BOCs' "local transportation" facilities. Consumers could make local calls to others attached to the cable system, as well as use the system to transmit a call to, or receive calls from, an inter-LATA carrier.

While a PUC might be able to refuse certification to a cable system to provide local and intrastate telephone service, it could not preclude use of the system for carrying interstate calls to inter-LATA carriers. Enforcing a prohibition on use of the facility to make local as well as long-distance calls within the state could again prove difficult once the system is established to provide interstate service.

Even if the BOCs can successfully identify and block only intrastate calls, the FCC may be able to preempt PUC efforts to confine the use of competing "local transportation" facilities to interstate services. When the FCC allowed subscribers to purchase and use their own telephones, the North Carolina PUC passed a regulation that prohibited their use for intrastate calls. Only telephones supplied by franchised telephone companies could be used to make both interstate and intrastate calls.

The FCC preempted the North Carolina regulation. The preemption was upheld in the courts because the state regulation, while formally restricting intrastate commerce, also affected the development of interstate commerce because it gave the telephone companies an unwarranted competitive advantage. Allowing BOCs to use their "local transportation" facilities for both interstate and intrastate communications, while confining competing facilities to interstate communications, could also be regarded as improper state interference with interstate commerce.[6]

PUCs' attempts to preserve telephone service monopolies within their states, or to force prices for particular services far above their costs, will likely not be successful over the long run. Their efforts can, however, impede the development of intrastate competition and the transition to cost-based prices in the short run. Given some PUCs' historic resistance to both trends in the provision of interstate service, some may attempt to prevent similar intrastate trends from developing after divestiture.

An alternative course of action that other PUCs may choose is careful analysis of BOC costs in providing "local transportation" service within each LATA. In doing so, they would determine the cost of providing such service for local, in-state, as well as out-of-state calls within a LATA, because the cost of providing that service does not differ according to the purposes for which it is provided. This is as true in telephone service as it is in transportation service. If we take a bus to the airport, the cost is the same whether we end our trip at that point or take a plane to another city within the state, or in another state. The price is also the same. The price for "local transportation" of a telephone call also should be the same whether it is ultimately an interstate, intrastate "toll" or local call, because the cost is the same.

In recent years, a number of PUCs have ordered (or permitted) the "unbundling" of local service rates for the purpose of aligning those rates more closely with costs. For example, states have ascertained the costs to provide local directory assistance ("information") service, to install service to a new customer, or to change service. Separate charges have been established to cover these costs, which apply only to customers who take the services. Moreover, optional lower-priced local services are available in a number of states. For example, for a relatively low monthly rate, a consumer may be able to make a few local calls, but the customer pays a separate charge for each additional call.

If PUCs continue this process, they are likely to find that flat rate local service is far too great a bargain at current prices. The service is roughly equivalent to a monthly pass to ride the local bus or subway system for as long as you wish, and as many times as you wish. While some people may want such service, they probably ought to pay a substantial price for it. Passes for a limited number of local "trips" could, of course, be made available at a lower price. For a lower flat monthly rate, packages of 10, 20, etcetera, local "trips" might be sold.

Many people would probably choose to pay for each call they make. Their unvarying monthly rate would then cover only the costs of providing them with access to the telephone network.

If all PUCs fashion telephone rates in this manner, BOC prices for making calls within a LATA—whether to another subscriber or to an inter-LATA carrier for delivery to another LATA—should ultimately be the same. Any intra-LATA competition for the BOCs that develops within a state as a result should be welcome, for an intra-LATA competitor would be offering service at rates that are competitive with the BOCs' actual costs. This would be efficient and effective competition. If the BOCs' rates for intra-LATA service are held above its costs, any competition that is allowed will be inefficient. Conversely, below cost BOC rates will discourage the development of efficient competition.

A PUC's decision between attempts to preserve monopoly and the power it provides to manipulate prices, on the one hand, and a systematic effort to align prices with costs and to permit competition, on the other hand, will not be made in a vacuum. As a result of the divestiture, the considerable costs incurred to provide subscribers with access to the telephone network have been isolated in the BOCs. The regular monthly rates subscribers now pay to the BOCs cover only some of these costs. A PUC that chooses to align price with cost, as the FCC has mandated, will have to permit increases in monthly rates in the short run. Any competition that develops as a result should hold these prices in check over the long run.

A PUC that attempts to preserve a monopoly may avoid increases in monthly rates in the short run, but may forego the benefits of competition that might emerge in the longer run. Constituent groups, through their elected and appointed representatives, will undoubtedly oppose short-run increases in their monthly service rates and remind the PUCs that the only thing we can be sure of in the long run is that we will all be dead.

CONCLUSION

Unlike the FCC, many PUCs had not yet faced the fundamental choice between monopoly and competition at the time that the AT&T divestiture decision was announced in 1982. While a number of PUCs had opposed the FCC's efforts to promote competition for interstate services, few had contemplated competition for the intrastate calls that fell within their jurisdiction. Divestiture forces them to face the issue. Their decision is likely to determine the role they will play in governing the telephone industry.

A decision in favor of regulated monopoly is not likely to hold up over the long run, because it could interfere with competition for interstate services. That interference would provide grounds for federal preemption. A process of continuing preemption of state decisions designed to preserve monopoly would eventually reduce the PUCs to an insignificant role in the development of government telecommunications policy.

This would be an unfortunate outcome. Many PUCs already have the resources and expertise to contribute to the development of an effective, long-run policy for a competitive telecommunications industry. Federal preemption of more and more PUC authority may well require replacement of that expertise in the short run by regional federal offices. The total cost of government involvement in the telephone industry would probably increase as a result.

Moreover, federal policy alone would then influence the pace of change and innovation in the industry. Under the current system of federal/state governance, individual PUCs are able to develop their own policies, as long as they are generally consistent with federal policy, as "experiments" within their states.[7] The New York PUC, for example, approved a simple, relatively cheap device for interconnecting customer-owned telephones in New York at a time when federal policy required more expensive and complex devices. Partly as a result of New York's favorable experience with its device, the FCC eventually liberalized its own national requirements. PUC experiments of this kind, particularly those which promote competition, would be foreclosed by federal preemption of the entire field.[8]

If the PUCs develop policies generally consistent with an industry-wide competitive regime, the FCC will have no reason to preempt PUC policies, preserving an important policy role for state regulation. The FCC would undoubtedly welcome the opportunity to share with the PUCs the burden of realigning prices with costs in the industry. In fact, insofar as rates for "local transportation" service are concerned, the PUCs are probably better able than the FCC to determine individual BOC costs within a LATA.

There are well over 100 BOC LATAs throughout the country. It would be difficult for a single federal agency to analyze the cost of "local transportation" in all of them. For the PUCs, however, it could be a manageable state-by-state effort.

If the FCC ultimately has to preempt most telephone ratemaking responsibility, it may be forced to rely on a broad cost average to keep the task manageable. This would be an unfortunate policy for an industry that may be evolving to fully deregulated status because of increasing competition. Without regulation, prices are likely to diverge from broad cost averages, as they did in the airline industry when airline rates were deregulated. A smoother transition from price regulation to deregulation would probably occur if deaveraging of prices began while they were still being regulated.

It would undoubtedly be easier for the PUCs to play an effective role in the development of a competition policy for the industry if monthly rates for telephone service were not going to increase in the short run. But adverse consumer reaction to rising monthly telephone rates can probably be minimized. The FCC is, in effect, requiring AT&T and the OCCs to make small contributions to a "universal service fund," the revenues from which will be used to subsidize the high costs of providing subscriber access in rural areas. Congress or state legislatures could provide similar programs, funded by income tax revenues, to assure that poor people in urban areas can afford access to the telephone network.

Of course, over the long run, programs of this type may not be necessary. If effective competition develops throughout the industry, it may spur enough technological innovation and productivity improvements to keep the cost of access to communications networks well within the reach of virtually all consumers. It is this long run prospect that should ultimately convince the PUCs, as it convinced the FCC, to develop policies fostering efficient and effective competition in the telephone industry.

NOTES

1. Kohlmeier, Louis M., Jr., *The Regulators*, Harper & Row, 1969, p. 93.

2. Certain parts of the country are served by independent telephone companies rather than Bell Operating Companies. Most of these independent company areas will be "parts" of BOC LATAs. The independent company will join the BOC to provide "local transportation" service. In a few areas, an independent company will provide the service alone, while the independent companies are not affected in the same manner as the BOCs by the divestiture. This chapter, for the sake of simplicity, does not attempt to cover the differences.

3. But PUCs cannot "disallow" prudently incurred costs necessary to provide telephone service. Telephone companies have the same constitutional protection as other corporations against government expropriation of their property. Moreover, they are not immune to inflation in their costs of doing business.

4. United States v. American Tel. & Tel. Co., 552 F. Supp. 159, fn. 117. (D.D.C. 1982).

5. The FCC's decision is contained in its *Third Report and Order* in Docket 78–72, Phase I (FCC 82–579), adopted December 22, 1982. The basic policy decision was affirmed, with certain revisions to the rules implementing the policy, in *Order on Reconsideration* (FCC 83–356), adopted July 27, 1983. These orders have been appealed by several parties, including the PUCs' organization, the National Association of Regulatory Utility Commissioners (NARUC) NARUC v. FCC, Cases 83 1225, et al., (D.C. Cir. 1983).

6. The FCC's preemption of the North Carolina regulation, and similar state regulations, was upheld in North Carolina Util. Com'n. v. FCC, 537 F.2d 787 (4th Cir.) *cert. denied*, 429 U.S. 1027 (1976).

7. In this role, the states are not merely serving the desires of their residents. Their individual initiatives often serve as models for subsequent national programs. Indeed, many of the federal laws we now take for granted as elements of a humane society were the product of state regulatory programs. As Justice Brandeis once observed: "It is one of the happy incidents of the federal system that a single courageous state may, if its citizens choose, serve as a laboratory; and try novel social and economic experiments without risk to the rest of the country." New State Ice Co. v. Liebman, 285 U.S. 262, 311 (Brandeis, J. dissenting).

8. For a discussion of this initiative and some others by the New York Commission, *see* A.E. Kahn and C.A. Zielinski, "New Rate Structures in Communications," *Public Utilities Fortnightly* (March 25, 1976) and "Proper Objectives in Telephone Rate Restructuring," *Public Utilities Fortnightly* (April 8, 1976).

8
COMPETITION AND UNIVERSAL SERVICE

Can We Get There From Here?

by Ithiel de Sola Pool

WHOM DOES ANTITRUST PROTECT?

Ten years from now, a substantial revisionist literature will undoubtedly have emerged lambasting the Consent Decree of 1982 as short-sighted and ill-considered.

As soon as late 1984 and 1985, there will be a torrent of protest against its short-term consequences. Homeowners will object to rate increases. People needing repairs will be puzzled as to where to turn. Extra digit dialing will be a nuisance. Stockholders will be bothered by having to make decisions regarding what to hold.

But it is not these difficulties of transition that I am talking about; those presumably will have been ironed out ten years from now. The criticisms that I anticipate are far more fundamental. They concern the basic premises of the divestiture decree. The fact that such criticism will exist will not prove the critics either right or wrong. All it will prove is that quick-freezing the realities of 1982 into a decree will not provide an appropriate arrangement for the technologies of 1992.

The policy decisions of Attorney General Baxter and Judge Greene are choices in a domain of tradeoffs; any benefits obtained by their decisions were won at substantial costs. In weighing the benefits against the costs, people's conclusions will differ depending on their personal values and factual predictions. But, one thing is clear: whatever benefits the new arrangements provide are being obtained at substantial costs. That is certainly not a unique feature of Baxter's or Greene's settlement; it would have been true for every alternative that was proposed. There were no neat solutions.

The scheme that was chosen has strong ideological roots in one particular justification of antitrust law and of competition. The underlying theory in the Department of Justice's proposed settlement was that the purpose of antitrust action is simply to ensure that market mechanisms will function. To put it differently, the underlying theory was that the persons being protected by antitrust law are those businesses which are actual or potential competitors in the marketplace. Under that theory, if a competitive market can be established, then the outcome is acceptable, whatever the outcome of that market may be for society as a whole. It follows that the government, as enforcer of the antitrust laws, is not concerned with the size of business units per se, nor with the service given the public.

Other theories as to what antitrust is all about look back at the history of the Grange movement and of the reform era out of which the Sherman Act grew. The abuses that stirred the reformers were exploitations of the public as much as of market competitors. High prices, discrimination in who was served, and manipulation of the political process by holders of great power were at least as important in legislation against trusts as were any theories about an ideal market structure.

The DOJ's theory was explicitly espoused by William Baxter in a journal article some years before he took public office.[1] In it he argued that only divestiture would prevent the phone company from cross-subsidizing local loops at the expense of business users of long-lines service. Antitrust policy, he felt, was to prevent social policy being followed at the expense of market-measured economic efficiency.

As a historical statement, that description of the purpose of antitrust law is, of course, specious. As a normative statement, it is a brief on behalf of one particular policy. In any case, it is the philosophy underlying the recent actions of the DOJ, the FCC, and Judge Greene's court.

The implementation of that philosophy leaves us with questions about what will happen to consumers of telecommunications service under an arrangement which has been designed to maximize one value, namely the efficiencies that a competitive market provides. There are tradeoffs to be examined between what has been achieved by creating that kind of market organization which economic theory and our society find generally desirable, and the resulting costs to some users of telecommunications service.

Let me emphasize that in insisting that we look empirically at the Decree's consequences for various classes of telecommunications users, I am not reaching a conclusion against the Decree nor against the use of market mechanisms. On the contrary, the case for introducing competition where possible is a strong one. I am only restating what sensible free market economists (in contrast to a small number of dogmatists) have always recognized, namely that the utility function a competitive market optimizes is not the only utility function. It does not measure every possible value.

A large economics literature deals with externalities, social costs, and the biases of using money as a measure of demand. We need not retread that ground. Adam Smith, himself, recognized that while the seeking of self-interest did under appropriate circumstances contribute to the wealth of nations, there was also a *Theory of Moral Sentiments* (the title of his other book) that applied to norms of sympathy which arise in situations such as family relations. He was not a dogmatist who believed the only measure of merit to be that which the market measures.

Nor was antitrust policy in America, we must repeat, historically a dogmatic embrace of market rationality. Notions of fairness were historically as important in the evolution of antitrust law as were economic doctrines. It was a policy concerned with the consequences of size and power as well as with competitive advantage. That, however, was not the perspective of the Department of Justice.

What exactly was it that the DOJ sought to achieve in a highly coherent and internally logical proposal? The basic objective of the DOJ's proposed settlement was to disjoin those markets in which they perceived monopoly to exist from those in which there was competition. No telecommunications vendor was to work in both. The DOJ believed the sole remaining domain of effective telecommunications monopoly was local exchange service, so the solution was to separate the vendors from all competitive activities. That would take care of the fundamental fear that profits from the monopoly could be used to cross-subsidize competitive activities. The validity of that approach was at best rather transitory and in any case was not adhered to consistently by Judge Greene.

There is good reason to believe that the recent erosion of the Bell monopoly that had occurred in long-distance service will occur in the next decade in local service, too. Cable systems, cellular radio, and other alternatives seem likely, perhaps within a decade, to make the rationale for the particular form of divestiture DOJ chose anachronistic.

But even if my prediction proves wrong, the Final Modified Judgment did not adhere to the DOJ's intended logic. The theory that it is important to prevent cross-subsidization from profitable monopolistic to inherently less profitable competitive markets implies that local exchange service should be a cash cow enabling AT&T (if there was no separation) to go into competitive markets with an unfair advantage. Ironically, the minute the Consent Decree was announced, the "wise men" of Wall Street declared to every reporter who would listen that AT&T had pulled off a coup, retaining for itself the promising competitive markets and sloughing off the burden of the marginally profitable regulated local exchange service.

There is a puzzle in all this. Both sets of platitudes cannot be simultaneously true. If the operating companies are the cash cow, they cannot simultaneously be losers that AT&T is happy to divest. What is important here, however, is not to argue where the truth lies, but to note that Judge Greene heard the alarms rung for the BOCs and gave them the benefit of some competitive activities in order to enhance their income stream. So in the end there is no consistent logic to what was assigned to whom, although the main structure proposed by the DOJ remains intact.

It is not the purpose of this paper to start the revisionist debate as to whether the DOJ logic represented a good or bad idea for public policy, whether Judge Greene's pragmatic modifications were desirable or not, or whether fragmentation of the unified monopoly was sound or not. It is just as well that I do not have to address these fundamental questions because I am not sure that I know the answers.

Here we need only explore a much narrower question, namely what the divestiture will do to some aspects of consumer service. What effects may we expect in regard to "universal service," the development of electronic mail, the balance between local and long-distance activities, and the long-run effect of the changed structure of communications carriage on related communications industries?

UNIVERSAL SERVICE

From its earliest days, the Bell System's goal and expectation was that telephone service should ultimately be available to everyone in the nation. Graham Bell greeted automatic exchanges with the ecstatic forecast that they would "so reduce the expense that the poorest man cannot afford to be without this telephone."[2] Two arguments have been made for a public policy that assures universal service: an equity argument for entitlement of all to phone service, and an externality argument that the aggregate value of communications to society is greater than the sum of what individuals in the market would individually pay.

The entitlement argument asserts that in a modern society telephonic communication, like education, basic medical care, and postal service, is an inherent attribute of citizenship. No one, no matter how poor, this argument asserts, should be denied the opportunity to phone for help in an emergency or be denied the participation in the life of the community that the telephone provides. That argument is used on behalf of lifeline service and for subsidized rural service. An example of this view is the inclusion of telephone subscriptions in the normal budget of welfare recipients. A job seeker should, our society believes, have access to a phone so as to be reachable by an employer with a job to offer. A parent should be able to call a doctor. A phone is defined as a necessity, not a luxury.

At least as common as the entitlement argument is the externality argument. When a person decides to subscribe to telephone service, he or she is revealing that the value of that service to him or her is greater than its price. In making such a decision to subscribe or not to do so, a poor person is, however, also affecting the value of phone service for others who may occasionally wish to phone the poor person. Social workers, salesmen, relatives, employers, and others get more value from their phones when they can reach everyone. It therefore makes sense for other telephone users to pay something to encourage subscription by fellow citizens who might otherwise be unable to subscribe. There is thus a social benefit to others when an added person subscribes to phone service. Those who benefit, not just the new subscriber, may be expected to pay for that.

An example of how universality of service benefits society (and not just the marginal user) is a problem that may exist during the process of shifting from hard-copy mail to electronic mail. Until virtually everyone has an electronic mail terminal, the Postal Service has to continue with hard-copy mail, delivered at ever larger unit costs as the volume of residual letters handled by the system falls. At some point it will pay for the government (or the electronic mail users) to buy off the remaining hard-copy mail users by giving them terminals.

Some economists have argued that in a strict sense the benefits that others gain when marginal subscribers sign up need not be viewed as an externality (as the word is used in economics), since charges for phone service could be so levied as to recapture the value that these third parties gain from added subscribers. If value-of-service pricing is used, phone tariffs to the subscribers could be set higher when 90% of households are on the network than when only 50% were.[3] We need not concern ourselves, however, with whether in economic jargon the word "externality" should be applied. Whatever word we use, the facts are as just described; the beneficiaries when new subscribers join the network are not just the new subscribers, but also the old ones who can now phone more people. It may well be that the most efficient way to collect appropriate charges from incidental beneficiaries is for the government to tax everyone and then subsidize phone service for those who would otherwise find it too expensive to subscribe to on their own.

In the United States, before the 1982 Consent Decree, the telephone monopoly handled the "externality" problem by cross-subsidization. Under the Ozark plan it charged too much for long-distance service, which is largely used by businesses and affluent subscribers, and transferred surplus funds to the local operating companies which charged less than cost for home use of local service.

Under the Consent Decree that will no longer be possible. The loss of an easy way to engage in desired cross-subsidization is one of the costs of the

1982 Consent Decree. If, as some critics are warning us, universal service becomes impossible in a competitive telephone market, then the losers will be not only those who have no phones, but also the rest of society.

We should not, however, uncritically accept the familiar argument that competition necessarily involves abandoning the goal of universal service. It is undoubtedly harder to assure universality of service under competition than it is where a monopoly can cross-subsidize without danger to itself. There do remain, however, other policy tools to achieve the same result. After all, our society does assure universal provision of food, shelter, education, and health care without establishing a monopoly in any of those fields.

To maintain universality of phone service in a competitive environment puts heavier reliance than in the past on such mechanisms as compulsory interconnection, shared directory services, common standards, and provision of subsidies.

The practice of compelling carriers to interconnect with their competitors has a long history in the United States. Telegraph companies, before Western Union achieved a monopoly, were required to take traffic for forwarding from each other on the same terms as they took it from any other customer.[4] The same principle had been applied to railroads and the same principle applies to banks. Although they do compete, they have to accept transactions from each other.

Ever since the 1968 *Carterfone* decision required AT&T to interconnect with an independent mobile radio service, the principle has been clear, at least for AT&T. Although various cases such as that with MCI (which is still in court) have turned upon the charge that equal interconnection was refused in practice, the principle is clear, and the penalties for its violation have been severe. Indeed, it is arguable that if AT&T had been more scrupulous in meeting the requirement for nondiscriminatory interconnection, the recent antitrust case and the divestiture following it would never have happened. The requirement for full interconnection has proven moderately enforceable and the consequences of attempting to avoid it quite severe.

So interconnection can be required among multiple servers in a network. But it could be that many of the competing networks ten years hence will argue, as telegraph companies used to, that they are not holding themselves out as common carriers, that they are offering only a specialized service, and that they should not be compelled to interconnect. AT&T Communications is not likely to be able to make such an argument. It has been a common carrier from the start and has been treated as the carrier of last resort. Other common carriers such as MCI and Sprint could not have succeeded had there been no universal carrier for customers to fall back on in locations to which OCC lines did not extend.

The fact that the Bell System has offered a universal service to which the OCCs could interconnect has made their operation practical. How will the system work if there is no Bell System to fall back on, and if routing between pairs of subscribers requires finding what company each subscriber is served by, and then linking these separate carriers, perhaps through intermediaries?

For such a system to work requires, at a minimum, cooperative directory, billing, and collection systems. To route a message, a subscriber to company A needs to be able to find a subscriber belonging to company B. There have to be intercompany agreements on how the charges would be billed and settled.

There are a number of examples of substantially simpler systems of this kind. For the airline reservation system, the consolidated guide gives information on what lines serve what routes, thus allowing connections to be made; and a settlement system allows phone companies in different countries (and for that matter the domestic independents) to route calls among each other by consulting the directory assistance operators in the target area. Nothing, however, is as complex as a competitive multicompany telecommunications network, if not even knowledge of the place to which the call is going will identify what company a particular customer uses.

The problem is not insoluble. But it will require computer information handling of a very high order and also substantial agreement among the carriers on the methods to be used for directory searches and for payments. AT&T can certainly not be expected to provide long-distance directory service free for the benefit of its competitors.

Agreements on such matters will constitute but a small subset of the standards that have to be set to make competitive telecommunications systems effective and, at the same time, universal. Technical standards are important in many industries as a means of assuring safety and economies of mass production, and to facilitate maintenance. Standards are particularly vital in those industries that create networks among customers; the whole point of such a facility is linkage. In the case of most commodities, a customer can be satisfied if the product that he buys is of good quality. If he buys a frying pan, he need not care about the quality of other frying pans as long as his works.

Communications is not like that. The quality of service for any one customer is, as we have seen, a function of how well that service interconnects with other parts of the network.

Telecommunications shares this crucial dependence on agreed standards with other networked systems. The monetary system works only if there is universal acceptance of the currency. The road system depends on universally accepted standards of design. Medical practice seeks not only to cure each individual patient, but also to protect society by stopping contagions from spreading from those who are sick.

Noting the variety of networked systems in which universal acceptance of standards is important brings home the lesson that while standards are important, the industry need not necessarily be organized as a monopoly. Banking, transportation, and health systems are very disaggregated, but somehow agreements have been reached that allow coordination despite disaggregation.

I wish it were possible at this point to say something profound about the requirements for future telecommunications standards based on some general theoretical analysis of the nature of standards. Unfortunately, no good theory of standards exists. You will find no serious treatment of the subject in economics, political science, or anywhere else. There are people who can talk wisely from experience about the problems of particular standards, but there is no general theory which deals with the question of when standards are desirable and when they are premature. There is no general theory about how one calculates the costs and benefits of uniform standards.

All that we can say is that there is a tradeoff between positive values of having standards (i.e., allowing interconnection, permitting economies of scale, facilitating maintenance in the field) and the negative consideration of inhibiting innovation by barring variation in the character of the product. One can also note that there is a proper timing of standards. Early in the life cycle of a product it may be desirable to avoid inhibiting innovation and variation. Later, when one variant of a product design has won market acceptance, it may be desirable to turn that *de facto* standard into a well-formulated agreement. The issue about standards for network services is less often whether a standard is ultimately desirable than whether it is premature.

Until now in the telecommunications field there have generally been two sets of standards, the CCITT standards of the International Telecommunications Union followed in most of the world and the Bell System standards which prevailed in America (about half the world market). In the future competitive environment, that situation may well change. The *de facto* leadership of AT&T and Bell Labs will undoubtedly remain in the U.S., although in reduced form.

Given the convergence of telecommunications with computing, IBM and perhaps other electronics companies will play an increased role in communications standards. Furthermore, the divested operating companies, the major independents, and large telecommunications users will be buying more of their equipment from companies other than Western Electric. Also, AT&T International will be seeking to sell Bell equipment abroad. So CCITT standards will become more influential in this country, and AT&T will have an incentive to reduce its deviations from them.

The pluralism and diversity of products that may result from this thrashing around will probably favor innovation, which is one of the things the divestiture was intended to achieve. But it will also make product choice harder for customers. Vendors of communications equipment will make strategic use of equipment characteristics and standards in their marketing. On the one hand, competitive challengers will be selling "AT&T compatible" equipment just as computer companies now make "IBM plug-compatible" equipment. On the other hand, vendors with some specialized market dominance will seek to incorporate in their products non-standard elements precisely to lock their customers out from competitive offerings by others.

We already see the beginning of this in band width differences in voice channels offered by competing long-distance carriers. The problem will be particularly acute when compression techniques use coding schemes that are incompatible with certain message formats.

Resolving problems of that sort will require the redefinition of the lines between common carriers and private networks. Companies will often define their service as a limited one, so as to avoid obligations of being a common carrier. While competition may make it less necessary to regulate tariffs of common carriers, public utility commissions and the FCC may wish to insist on non-discriminatory interconnection so as to assure universal service to the public. But a specialized carrier may often claim that the technical parameters of the service it offers (such as those for compression) make it impossible to interconnect economically with certain other networks.

That is not a specious claim. One way to provide an economically attractive service is to adapt it narrowly to a particular use. But that raises the question of who bears the responsibility of assuring universal basic service.

For that problem, the only solution is to frankly recognize the need to subsidize or cross-subsidize some users, to provide basic service. We have already noted that it is economically justified to charge the beneficiaries of the "externality" of universality in order to subsidize users who would otherwise opt out of the system. We now need to consider who may need to be subsidized and how.

The usual example of a service that needs subsidization is that for rural areas. Congress certainly had that in mind in its deliberations about a fund to assure affordable universal service. In fact, however, it may not turn out to be a very good example. In the past, when wire lines were almost the sole method of reaching the customer's premises, the argument was valid that without cross-subsidization, phone companies would not serve remote rural locations.

Today, however, radio communication offers alternatives that make rural service quite affordable with little or no subsidization. The capital cost of stringing wire to an isolated farmstead is such that, with cost-based tariffs, many farms would be forced to do without phone service. But with the same sort of equipment that is used for mobile radiophones (or in the future a voice grade satellite link), no farm need be so far from a concentrator or switch as to be deprived of phone service, with at most a relatively modest subsidy.

More to the point is the concern that there be a low lifeline tariff for the very poor. Other candidate services for subsidy, because they meet social needs, are emergency numbers that can be called without a coin from phone booths, educational uses of broad band services (such as CATV), special phones and terminals for the deaf, and automatic monitoring terminals for the aged.

The natural candidate organization to provide such service is the local phone operating company. As long as that remains a monopoly, as the Consent Decree assumes it is, such cross-subsidization seems appropriate, provided other tariffs are set at a level to grant a fair return to the system as a whole.

However, operating companies are no longer fully protected monopolies. The threat of bypass hangs over their heads. Charging more for business service than it truly costs is a sure way to encourage the bypass business.

These considerations lead to the usual conclusion of economists about subsidies, namely that an explicit subsidy is preferable to a hidden subsidy. If government authorities are anxious that there be a lifeline service offered below true cost, then a subsidy to offset the loss would be the most economically efficient procedure.

Being a political scientist rather than an economist, I am not persuaded that the best form of subsidization is always the explicit one. That may be the best way to get economic efficiency, but it is often not the best way to assure political tranquility. There is a lot to be said for a practice such as exists in CATV, franchising under which the seeker of a franchise takes the initiative in making the most appealing set of promises that he can think of, rather than a practice in which political bodies debate what to put into the budget as an explicit subsidy.

The cable franchise model allows for more decentralized decision-making and also for decision-making by the people most intimately involved in the practical matter of offering service. Hidden subsidies are often good political solutions in a world of tensions.

However, in a competitive marketplace in which, if the carrier is to survive, tariffs must reflect costs, the hidden subsidy option may not exist. In the post-divestiture environment, government agencies that wish to have unprofitable communications services offered will have to get into the habit of paying part of the cost out of the treasury. Needless to say, that will not be an easy political process.

If the above forecasts turn out to be even partly accurate, there may be a substantial change in the role and power of public utility commissions. Under the previous monopoly regime, their main function was to police tariffs.

Other functions dealt with safety and engineering approval of capital investments; these all concerned the internal management of the carrier. The
PUC, if it did its job well, was the citizen's eyes. But those eyes were trained
narrowly on the single carrier's way of doing business.

In the new competitive regime, many of the jobs that the PUC did in the
past will be turned over to the market for decision. But some public policy
decisions will remain that deal with relations among different companies,
such as who are to be common carriers and how are public funds to be spent
for obligatory social services. The arena of political debate about telecommunications policy is likely to broaden at the very time that the specialized
regulatory agencies concerned with telecommunications abandon much of
their previous responsibility.

THE IMPACT OF SHIFTING
LOCAL/LONG DISTANCE RATES

A regime in which tariffs move toward true costs will have some effect on
the geographical organization of enterprises. As local rates rise and long-
distance rates fall toward a distance-insensitive tariff structure, it will pay
increasingly to do things from a distance. For most organizations and enterprises, communications costs are a significant, but far from a dominant,
item. One should therefore not anticipate that shifts in communications
costs will produce revolutionary changes in the locales of business.

Yet changes will gradually occur. People will find themselves increasingly
talking and sending electronic messages all over the country, thus building
relationships and drawing on information services without regard to where
the data happen to be stored.

A probably incorrect forecast that one often hears is that cheap long-
distance communication will reduce travel. On the contrary, travel is more
likely to increase, since relationships established by telecommunications will
often lead to a need for the parties to meet. Nonetheless, an overall reduction in the cost of carrying on activities from a distance will ultimately be
reflected in how activities come to be placed in tables of organization. It may
become quite normal to put a large clerical staff in a place chosen for low
rents and for availability of the right kind of labor, even if it is half the
country away from its corporate headquarters. Just as factory facilities are
now located without reference to the location of headquarters or sales offices, so white collar centers may migrate to spots determined by considerations quite other than the need to communicate.

The 1982 Consent Decree may contribute to the trend toward increased
geographic dispersion of activities. Increasing competition forces tariffs

toward costs, and for long-distance communication these costs are falling. However, the trend toward flat rates regardless of distance will reach a limit under the new structure.

The LATA structure is likely to introduce some rather uncomfortable discontinuities in the cost/distance relationships. Even if inter-LATA rates became completely distance-insensitive, then local and access charges at the two ends plus that flat long-distance charge would be the rate for a long-distance call to any extra-LATA point.

It is obvious that under that rate structure, there is a strong incentive for a large communications user to bypass the local charges. Rooftop antennas for direct satellite or DTS service are likely to mushroom. Transferring the access charge to the bill for the local terminal does not (despite what the FCC seems to believe) change that fact. It only changes the games heavy users have to play. They then have to reduce their chargeable terminals by gimmicks that get terminals off the main network, although privately interconnected with it.

There is no way in which an artificial organizational distinction between local and long-distance service can be imposed without causing large sophisticated telecommunications users to design their system so as to save money under the rules. If the rules change, the responsive strategies will always exist. Since the technology for local and long-distance communication is likely to become less distinct than in the past, a decree designed to keep them distinct is an inevitable target for evasion.

To combat bypass arrangements by large organizations, operating companies will try to keep business charges down. Since residential users are not easily able to migrate to bypass service, the natural trend of residential local charges to rise to their real costs may be further stimulated.

Indeed, that is exactly how a monopoly carrier should charge under the theory of Ramsey pricing. The charges should be inverse to the elasticity of the customer's demand so as not to drive away marginal customers. Big users can invest in devices to reduce their use of the carrier's service, but the ordinary citizen cannot; the rational pricing policy is to reduce charges for the big customer and raise them for the citizen. This is not likely to be a politically appealing outcome.

NEW SERVICES

One major effect of the Consent Decree will be to put some new strong actors into the business of offering competitive information services. Among the most lucrative new services may be electronic mail, videotex, electronic funds transfer, billing, teleconferencing, and CATV.

In addition to these, there is a set of services that before the divestiture were extensively discussed as likely parts of an integrated services digital network (ISDN). These included call forwarding and numbers assigned to individuals instead of just to phones. The latter group of ISDN-related services (some based on the common-control switching network) are likely to be somewhat delayed by divestiture because many of them, like national call forwarding, require close cooperation of the local and long-distance companies. It may take some time to work out how (given that the operating company is not supposed to discriminate between AT&T and its competitors) these services, which are quite integral to the network itself, will be managed.

The former group of services, including electronic mail, videotex, etcetera, may be accelerated by the divestiture because those are services that rest on the network but are not as deeply integrated into it. Most of them are value-added activities that can be offered by independent vendors using leased lines or switched service. (Video is a special case because of its band width requirements.)

The new structure of the telephone industry means that in addition to specialized VANs, these services may also be offered by American Bell, GTE, and the divested operating companies. The latter have to ask permission of the court, but are likely to get it, and in some instances even for activity outside the geographic area in which they provide local switching service.

Electronic mail services are already here to a large degree, and they are using the telephone network. Most of it is intracompany. For electronic mail to begin to take over in intercompany correspondence and in communication to and from the home, several developments are necessary. First, there must be a universal address or directory system. The phone companies are in a good position to offer that. Secondly, terminals must be disseminated that conform to standards, so that they are mutually compatible. Such standards will not be agreed to easily, but again, the phone companies are in a good position to take the lead. Third, a system of charging must be developed. For that, too, the phone companies are in a position to use their established facilities.

Electronic funds transfer is a special form of electronic mail. Money after all, is nothing but a "note." However, it requires more security features on the network than does correspondence, and so it is likely to be a separate system.

Electronic mail is a common carrier activity which phone companies could undertake without running afoul of the Consent Decree. Videotex, on the other hand, does have major restrictions on it. While phone companies could offer to provide the transmission service, they are barred by the Consent Decree from going into the content side of the business. (I question the constitutionality of that restriction, but do not expect any of the phone companies to go to court to challenge it.)

Videotex in the United States may end up being a highly competitive business. Since the transmission of videotex is undertaken by a common carrier, all it takes to become a videotex publisher is to have some useful data on a computer. Such a publisher can provide service to anyone who dials his number.

However, without an automated billing facility it would be hard to make that kind of publishing profitable. A phone company can offer a publisher that. So can cablecasters, and they have more bandwidth to offer. There may well be significant competition between phone and cable companies for videotex delivery and associated billing services.

The telephone system already provides audio teleconferencing, but it has not chosen to balance the bridge connections. Other entrepreneurs have therefore found that it is a value-added business they can provide. Video teleconferencing and other video services will be natural for telephone companies to offer to their customers once the installation of optical fiber runs far enough down the network to reach at least a nearby concentrator, if not the customer's phone itself. That will take some time, and in the meantime, cable systems have an advantage in the video market.

In the end, however, there is likely to be head-to-head competition between telephone and cable networks in offering video to users. It seems unlikely that the present federal regulations barring a phone company from offering cable service in locations where it offers phone service can last.[5] What is more likely to be an issue with regard to phone companies, as it now is with cable companies, is the desire of some phone companies to get into the profitable programming end of the cable business. At present that would be barred by the Consent Decree's provision against engaging in mass media business.

Even if that restriction survived a constitutional test, it is likely to fall before the wave of deregulation and the logic of a competitive market. However, if phone companies departed from their common carrier tradition and restricted who put what video on the optical fiber broad band network, the public and the government would be unlikely to sit still. An attempt by phone systems to preempt program control (as the cable systems are now trying to do) would in all probability bring regulation down on them once more.

We can thus anticipate that in the era in which the 1982 Consent Decree reigns, a complex set of offerings will be offered to users. The various phone companies will in some fields be the dominant vendors, in others they will play a less important role. In value-added services each phone company will be just one of a number of competitors, and some of these competitors will be other phone companies. Deregulation is likely to continue to free phone companies from some of the remaining restrictions, such as the one against media activities, but it would take very little by way of "unfair" competition, denying competitors use of telecommunication facilities, to bring regulation back again.

CHANGES IN INFORMATION INTERMEDIARIES

The relationship between carriers and the services which they deliver is one issue that was supposed to be resolved in the Consent Decree, but which will keep coming up in the future. A major objective of both the FCC and the Decree has been to allow AT&T into a wider range of business activities than had been allowed under the 1956 Decree. It was widely felt in the government and by independent analysts that it was no service to the public to keep this talented hi-tech company from contributing fully to the electronic revolution.

But late in the process of unleashing AT&T, the newspaper publishers suddenly realized that this would mean a new competitor for them, specifically with regard to the want ads. They promptly organized a campaign to bar telephone companies from engaging in publishing, and succeeded in getting such a restriction into the Modified Final Judgment for at least seven years.

Quite aside from whether the newspaper publishers were right or wrong in regard to principles of free speech and First Amendment law (a matter on which I have written elsewhere),[6] they were certainly right in perceiving that electronic information delivery may vastly change the structure of the present information industries and institutions.

In general, institutions are built around scarcities of one sort or another, which can be called bottlenecks. If a resource is totally abundant, like the air that we breathe, no one can organize the provision of it in such a way as to make money. At the other extreme, if a much-wanted resource can be totally monopolized by some organization, then that organization can gain great power and wealth. The ordinary intermediate situation is that an entrepreneur succeeds in gaining some limited advantage in provision of a resource (be it something as trivial as a convenient location for his store), and by virtue of that strategic advantage he builds his firm or institution.

In the information field, the thing that customers are seeking is some knowledge or entertainment. That content in itself can rarely be controlled. As has often been noted, words and ideas, once they are released, are out of control of their imparter. What can be controlled to a limited extent are some of the physical facilities by which the information is processed, transmitted, or stored. It is around these bottlenecks that information enterprises and institutions are built. Among crucial institutions are publishers, broadcasters, studios, theaters, libraries, schools, universities, and banks. Until the last few decades the great bulk of information was provided in hard copy. The bottlenecks that could be controlled had to do with the supply of paper, printing on it, distributing the printed product, and storing it for later times. Figure 8.1 represents the basic structure of print-based institutions. Strategic leverage was in the hands of those who engaged in printing, publishing, distributing, and archiving the product. Out of this paper handling system grew the great intellectual institutions on which our culture is based: newspapers, magazines, book publishers, universities, and libraries. Certainly we who belong to intellectual occupations value these institutions enormously and do not wish to see them decay. Yet in an electronic age, the institutions will be different because the bottlenecks are different.

Figure 8.2 represents a speculation on the likely structure of information institutions in a mature electronic era. It is not that the demands of the ultimate user have changed (though that may happen too.) The ultimate user wants the substantive content consisting of facts, insights, and entertainment. These are provided by creative people. While changes may also be taking place in authoring as science and the arts progress and change their styles, the greatest and most obvious change is in the intermediary institutions that are built around the physical process of getting the information to the ultimate user.

The striking feature of Figure 8.2 is that only carriers remain in the strategic center of the process. As long as a carrier exists and is accessible, the nature of electronic distribution allows the ultimate user to have a direct relationship with the creator of the original information. That point is illustrated by interactive computer use. Only one intermediary institution, the carrier, is required to enable a user to reference the computer-stored files that some individual or group has created and then stored on its own computer. Interaction within a computer network becomes a highly individual, and often two-way pattern of interaction between the author's file and the reader's terminal.

We may anticipate substantial change in the print-based intermediary organizations portrayed in Figure 8.1, and indeed some erosion of them in their present form. Printing is likely to be done increasingly on-demand, in editions of one. Printing institutions will be much affected.

Computer-aided instruction will change universities in ways that will become apparent as we see the outcome of the Carnegie-Mellon, Brown, Drexel, Stevens and MIT experiments. Libraries will lose many functions as users get material by reading it over telecommunications lines from whatever computer it happens to be stored in, anywhere in the world.

Let us not overstate the case. There are many firms and institutions that

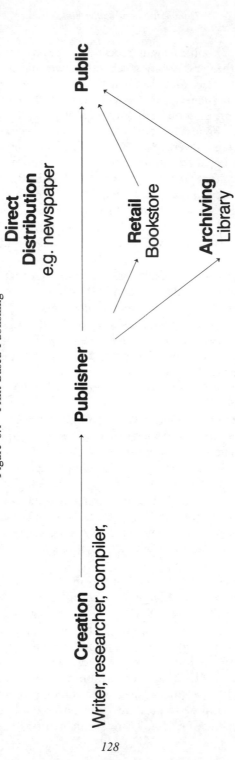

Figure 8.1   Print Based Publishing

Figure 8.2   Electronic Publishing

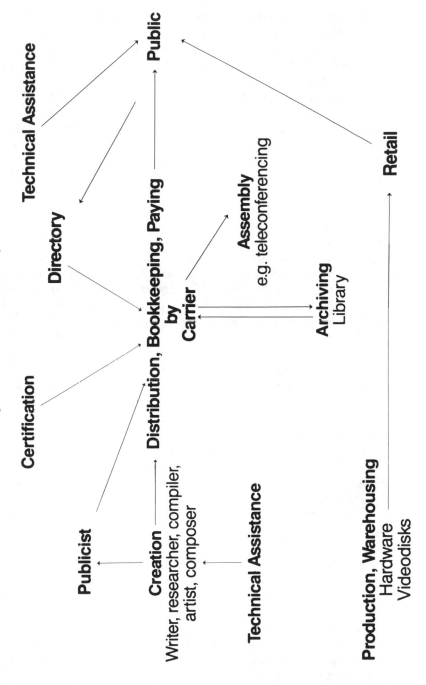

can and will grow up around this process of information dissemination in an electronic mode. There are publicists who do a part of the job that a present publisher does, namely advertise or otherwise publicize the availability of an information or entertainment file, where it is, and how to get it. There are programmers, teachers, and trainers who help the insufficiently skilled user of information technology learn how to make the machines work. There are repairmen who fix the terminal or computer when it ceases to work.

But none of these has the same degree of control of a bottleneck that the publisher has in creating and distributing the paper objects on which knowledge is embedded. If this analysis is correct, we are moving into a much more flexible, less bureaucratized information system in the electronic age, where market control elements will be weaker—with but one exception: carriers.

I use the word carriers in the plural because we see a rapidly growing set of competitors, including telephone, cable, microwaves, cellular radio, satellite circuits, broadcast subcarriers, and so on. Yet as we noted when we discussed universal service, lack of interconnection may cause bottlenecks in getting from node to node. There is less and less a problem of a monopoly carrier, but there are problems of access to the most convenient or economical carrier. There are also problems of interconnection.

The Consent Decree has affected some of these matters in a significant way. But in other respects, it has avoided crucial issues. The Consent Decree has multiplied the number of independent carriers. There never was the prospect, about which the newspaper publishers shouted, of a single monopoly publisher, but now after divestiture, that prospect is more remote than ever. The Consent Decree does deal with the problem of access to carriers in a very limited context, namely access of long-distance carriers to local switches. It does not address the problem in a more general way.

The testing ground for how society will deal with the need of authors, publishers, and users for access to carriers is likely to be in media other than the telephone. Cable systems, because they intermix programming and carriage in the same corporate containers, are likely to be the arena of greatest debate. Yet telephone systems are likely to get increasingly involved in some of the same issues.

AT&T has responded with remarkable flexibility to the challenge the government gave it to become a customer-oriented competitor. It is doing that job well. But inevitably the new mode of operation which the FCC and the Consent Decree have imposed on the company will impel it into situations where it becomes not only a carrier, but also a provider of service to the end users in competition with others who use it as a carrier.

The creation of American Information Systems, the fully separated subsidiary, was designed to cope with that problem. Nonetheless, it is in this range of issues that 10 or 15 years from now, when dissatisfaction with the continued relevance of the 1982 Consent Decree has become more wide-spread, in which I would expect the most acerbic of the new discussions of telecommunications policy will lie.

CONCLUSION

In drawing the conclusion that the 1982 Consent Decree will not be long viable as a solution acceptable to the American public, I am not suggesting that it cannot be defended as a good solution for 1982. Whether a cost/benefit analysis would say that that Decree or some alternative to it was the best answer to some current problems of the 1980s is not what this paper addressed. But if anyone believes that the present Decree will meet the fundamental needs of the public as they will appear in the 1990s, I must beg to dissent. The most fundamental problems have hardly been touched. The debate over communications policy will not be stilled. If it has been vociferous recently, it may well be more so a decade hence.

NOTES

1. "How Government Cases Get Selected," *American Bar Association Anti-Trust Journal*, Spring 1977, pp. 596–601.

2. Ithiel de Sola Pool, *Forecasting the Telephone: A Retrospective Technology Assessment*, Norwood, N.J.: Ablex Publishing Corp., 1983, p. 22.

3. Charles Jonscher, unpublished paper.

4. Ithiel de Sola Pool, *Technologies of Freedom*, Cambridge: Harvard University Press, 1983, pp. 91–98.

5. Eli M. Noam, "Toward an Integrated Communications Market: Overcoming the Local Monopoly of Cable Television," *Federal Communications Law Journal*, vol. 34, no. 2, Spring 1982, pp. 209–257.

6. Ithiel de Sola Pool, *Technologies of Freedom*, Cambridge: Harvard University Press, 1983, pp. 206–209.

9
THROUGH A GLASS BRIGHTLY

CONSUMERS AND THE NEW TOMORROW

by Linda Grant

"In ten years we'll all be glad we did this."[1]

For residential and business consumers, the breakup of the Bell System has unleashed a broad spectrum of reactions ranging from worries about the rising cost and continued reliability of telephone service to an enthusiastic embrace of the benefits expected to flow from the burgeoning world of high-tech communications.

Whether the response is nagging anxiety or optimism, however, one view is commonly shared: the transitional period will be a rocky one. Divestiture of the local operating companies from Ma Bell's formidable financial and technological market will radically alter the way telephone services in this country are offered and used. Those changes are likely to prove complex and perplexing until a period of testing—which various industry specialists estimate may take anywhere from two to ten years—has been completed and a host of troublesome issues resolved.

Central to evaluation of the divestiture's impact is the question of the financial health and viability of the seven regional operating companies that are being so abruptly severed from Ma Bell's protective umbrella. Only when those companies have convincingly demonstrated that they can thrive and prosper independently, at ease with their new competitive freedoms, will many gnawing doubts be erased.

Few people are worried about the operating companies' strength over the long haul. Professor Harry M. Trebing, director of the Institute of Public Utilities at Michigan State University, points out, "Their markets are growing rapidly, they have access to financial markets, and there are opportunities to use new technologies such as cellular radio. It's not like technology bypassed them—this is not a case of the pony express being replaced by the telegraph."[2]

Echoes Lee Selwyn, president of Economics & Technology Inc., a consulting firm in Cambridge, Massachusetts, "I'm not bothered by the health of the operating companies. I don't think it was in the national interest to have our entire communication system in control of a single entity. And I think any of the seven companies is going to be fully capable of operating on a sufficient scale."[3]

Nevertheless, the confusion surrounding divestiture and the companies' symbiotic reliance on state regulatory commissions have the potential for posing "an awful short-term problem," Prof. Trebing concedes.[4]

A similar view is expressed by Robert W. Nichols, legislative and regulatory counsel for Consumers Union in Washington, D.C., which represents residential and small-business users. Says Nichols, "We support divestiture. We think the end result will be favorable to both business and residential users. In ten years, we'll all be glad we did this. But I am concerned about the next ten years."[5]

Nichols believes business will see the positive results first. Already, the business community is far more mindful than residential consumers of the advantages to be gained from the technological advances and competition that have forced the shakeup of the telecommunications industry.

Says Kenneth Bosomworth, president of International Resource Development Inc., a Stamford, Connecticut, consulting firm, "Business will be the winner where telecommunications is used effectively to increase company growth, productivity and profitability. To the extent that a lot of competitive activity brings more benefits to business, divestiture is an extremely positive influence."[6]

Many businessmen agree with the judgment. Yet, they are uneasy about the short run. Reflecting the perspective of many big-business users, says Robert Bennis, manager of communications systems at Westinghouse Electric Co. and chairman of the public policy committee of the International Communications Association, "We are approaching this new era with guarded optimism. It will probably take at least 18 months to two years for all the major areas of confusion and concern to settle into place. I think we are in for a fairly chaotic 1984."[7]

Bennis stresses that the ICA endorses the concept of competition in telecommunications. But that philosophic agreement does not mitigate the deep concerns many members feel. "These basic changes are painful."[8]

For residential consumers—many of whom lack business's first-hand experience with the convenience and energy-saving advances offered by the new "smart" telephones—there is even greater distress over the impending changes.

Humorist Russell Baker captured some of the nation's uneasy spirit in his *New York Times* Sunday *Magazine* column "Sunday Observer" last year when he wrote, "The prospect of shopping for a telephone gives me a green rash. . . . One of the great things about the Telephone Company was . . . (that) you got the only phone on the market. The phone company's phone. There were no great bargains, no reason to shop carefully. . .and if the Telephone Company installed it, it was going to work beautifully or get fixed in jig time by the Telephone Company's crackerjack repair teams. It made life easier."[9]

THE COST ISSUE

Specific adjustments to the unfolding brave new world of telecommunications will differ for residential and business consumers. Costs for business are expected to drop, but residential consumers can anticipate paying more for local phone service. In part, that's because business was charged more before divestiture to help support basic service to homes.

Corporate customers are concerned that political pressure on state regulatory bodies to hold down those residential rates may cause the commissions to "sock it to business," in the words of one businessman, piling on as many extra charges as they think the market can bear. They are also worried that service might deteriorate if the commissions withhold necessary rate increases in order to appease protesting consumers.

Despite these fears, most businessmen predict that the commissions—after much agonizing—will have little choice other than to maintain adequate levels of service, even though that decision will require the politically unpalatable choice of hiking local rates.

One big unknown is what will happen to rates for intrastate calls, that is, those made within a state but between zones the phone companies call Local Access Transport Areas (LATAs). With divestiture, the nation will be divided into some 160 LATAs controlled by the operating companies, with states like California carved up into ten LATAs. While the Federal Communications Commission (FCC) will continue to regulate interstate LATA routes, state commissions will oversee traffic between LATAs within one state.

Some states, such as Florida and Texas, immediately authorized competition among their state LATAs by lower-priced long-distance companies such as GTE's Sprint or International Telephone & Telegraph's City Call II, a move designed to hold down costs. However, analysts believe that long-distance competitors will be interested only in skimming the cream of routes such as San Francisco to Los Angeles, or Dallas to Houston. Thus, prices for most intrastate calls could soar, while only those on dense routes drop.

Depending on the location of a company's facilities, the rise in intrastate rates could either be a serious penalty or a substantial boon. Businesses in California, for example, could be the winners where heavy traffic jams lines between cities in different LATAs such as Los Angeles, San Diego, and San Francisco.

Small business is also expected to escape much of the cost squeeze. Although local rates will climb, long-distance rates are projected to drop—a mix that should provide a net benefit to small concerns.

For residential customers, the major issue is the charge for local service. Local rates are the fixed monthly charge that a telephone owner must pay in order to get a dial tone, and which allow him to make calls within a specified distance. In California, for example, Pacific Telephone & Telegraph offers three different rates to cover calls made within an eight-mile radius—a minimum charge of $2.50 that allows 30 local calls and a maximum of $7.00 that allows unlimited phoning. Calls dialed up to 24 miles are billed like long-distance calls, based on time and distance, but are usually included in any discussion of local rates.

Says Susan W. Leisner, Florida Public Service commissioner and chairman of the state commissioners' divestiture committee, "The impact on the local ratepayer is the main concern with divestiture. We think it will be substantial."[10] She has testified that local rates in Florida are expected to double to $25 to $30 in two years. Other commissions have projected similar price hikes.

But just as small business may benefit from some of the changes, so may certain consumers who are heavy users of long-distance service. That group may enjoy an overall reduction in their total telephone bills after divestiture, if the decline in their toll-call costs more than offsets the big increase in local rates.

Analysts are divided on exactly how much responsibility for higher local rates should be blamed on divestiture. State regulatory officials, for example, attribute much of the anticipated jump to the reshaping of the Bell companies.

As evidence, they cite the huge rate increases requested by the operating companies during 1983, many of which were justified as necessary because of the then-impending divestiture. Commissioners worry such rate requests will proliferate again in 1984 because they fear the local companies will discover that their revenue is insufficient to support the assets they are assigned.

Consumers Union's Nichols argues the more moderate position, that divestiture "should have no direct impact on cost, although it might hasten some decisions and heighten awareness of change."[11] But he, too, fears that local companies will continue to justify rate hikes on the basis of divestiture because that explanation is easy and understandable. "Absent something like the Ayatollah in energy," he says, "they're in difficulty. Who wants to explain (complicated Federal Communications Commission) decisions on depreciation? But the nasty federal government that broke up Ma Bell is doing this to us . . . now that's an appealing argument."[12]

On the far end of the spectrum, Economics & Technology's Selwyn contends that divestiture cannot be isolated as a stand-alone event, because it follows logically from deregulation. "Deregulation creates the foundation for a breakdown of the subsidy system and averaging of rates," says Selwyn. "It also creates a change in the way equipment is depreciated. Those three factors account for the increase in costs."[13]

THE DEREGULATION ISSUE

Certainly the prices of various telephone services were destined to change substantially as a result of deregulation and competition in the telecommunications industry, a process which began nearly 30 years ago when the FCC first allowed certain companies to install their own microwave systems.

Deregulation gathered momentum in the 1970s, as competitors such as MCI began to offer long-distance service, pressuring AT&T to match lower rates. It became inevitable that the tangled skein of subsidies that had been built into the U.S. telecommunications system—which had served the national goal of installing universal service in more than 90 percent of all American homes—would eventually have to be unraveled.

That system had held long-distance rates at an artificially high level for decades. Although electronic technology was rapidly reducing the costs of calling far from home, federal and state regulators continued to favor a social policy of keeping those rates elevated in order to cover the rising costs of stringing wire to nearly every household, no matter how remote its location.

Moreover, rate-averaging kept the cost of communicating with thinly populated areas artificially low by maintaining the price of communications on heavily used routes artificially high. With competition, rate-averaging is bound to break down as competitors vie to price certain routes selectively. Economists point to airline deregulation to prove their point—it costs less today to fly from coast to coast, a densely traveled route, than from Pittsburgh to Gulfport, Mississippi.

In addition, extra income from leasing telephone equipment was destined to be lost when competition was allowed in the terminal equipment market. To prepare for that competition, the FCC had to radically revise the way equipment was depreciated. If AT&T was to keep pace with competitors in introducing new, high-tech features in its telephone, PBX, transmission, and switch equipment, it had to be allowed to write off that equipment over a much shorter period than in the old slow days of monopoly.

Before competition, equipment was depreciated over 12 to 20 years—an unusually long period set by regulators to limit costs to consumers. That policy had to change because with competition and high technology, equipment can become obsolete in far less time.

Thus, the FCC ruled that equipment which in the past might have been written off over 20 years could be recovered in 15. "That's a real dollar increase in the total cost of providing telephone service," says Selwyn.[14] He estimates that the real costs of a piece of equipment installed today, including inflation and a write-off over five years, could be as high as five to six times more costly than it was ten years ago.

Eventually, the economic policy to deregulate—embodied in various FCC decisions and court orders that granted AT&T's competitors more and more freedoms—overwhelmed the social policy to subsidize local telephone service. With the FCC's *Computer II* ruling, implemented in 1983, the die for dismantling the old system was cast. The main question that remained was how to ease the pain.

SOLUTIONS

Several plans to mitigate some of the discomfort have been proposed.

Access Charge

To offset lost revenue from the long-distance subsidy, the FCC proposed an access charge to be paid monthly by telephone subscribers, begun in 1984. The fee is a minimum of $2 for residential users and $4 for business consumers for the first year. But the sum increases over the next seven years to a maximum to be determined by a formula that takes into account such factors as inflation and the cost of new plant and equipment. Experts estimated in 1981 that it would require an average monthly charge of $7 to equal the amount now contributed by long-distance.

Critics of the plan, which include influential members of Congress, are concerned that it threatens universal service, because the formula passes the costs of long-distance access onto consumers regardless of whether they make toll calls. State commissioners, especially, fear that the poor, the elderly, or the handicapped—customers who are particularly dependent on telephones—may be forced to give up service because of the escalation expected in local-service rates. Responding to political pressure, the FCC announced in February 1984 that it would postpone implementation of the residential charge until 1985.

Unfortunately, no hard data suggest how many households would drop off the network at various price levels. However, Lewis J. Perl, senior vice president of the New York-based National Economic Research Associates Inc. has studied the impact on households of hypothetical increases of 50 percent, 100 percent, and 200 percent. Those represent monthly service-charge increases in basic service of $6.60, $13.20 and $26.40.

With a $6.60 increase, the Perl study indicates a decrease of 3.7 percent in telephone demand; at $13.20 the decrease is 8.6 percent; and at $26.40 the decrease is 22.5 percent. Says Perl, "Clearly, the effect of the monthly charges currently contemplated by the FCC would be much smaller."[15] He estimates that an access charge of $2 a month would decrease demand by less than 1 percent. A charge of $7 a month would result in a national average decrease of less than 4 percent.

State commissioners, of course, are worried about the total impact of all increases, not just the access charge. Thus, if the Florida Commission estimate was realized, according to Perl's data, a $12.50 to $15 a month increase over two years would result in about 8 percent to 10 percent of all subscribers ending service.

Universal Service Fund

To cap price hikes on consumers in costly locations, the FCC has devised a formula to begin in 1986. By this proposal, telephone companies will contribute a percentage of revenues from long-distance calls to a Universal Service Fund. The money will then be distributed to telephone companies through a formula based on their local costs.

Critics worry that the fund targets rural areas only and ignores big-city poor. For the urban poor, who are served by big companies unlikely to qualify for payments from the fund, other solutions are being studied. Telephone companies believe that one way to hold down their costs is to tailor bills more specifically to consumer usage.

Local Measured Service

To that end, the companies are trying to shift more and more residential local billing from a flat rate to a measured rate that calculates the number of calls placed each month and the price of each call based on its length, the time of day it is made, and the distance called (many business bills are already compiled on a measured basis).

According to AT&T and the independent telephone companies, the justification for switching to LMS, as "local measured service" is called, (GTE calls it USS for "usage-sensitive service") is to let consumers control costs. For many customers, the companies say, a small monthly local access charge plus low usage charges will save money over a flat rate.

The New York State Public Service Commission, which regulates the system with the highest penetration of measured service, agrees. Says Neil Swift, director of the communications division, "Our studies indicate that in Manhattan, about one-third of all subscribers would have smaller bills if they subscribed to the basic budget service offered with LMS. They either know that and don't care or don't know it. For some, it is a question of prestige."[16]

But Swift points out that in the past, budget service has been subsidized by long-distance service. Because that will no longer be the case, as a result of divestiture, he is unsure whether the costs of budget LMS service will be any lower than a flat rate. "Somebody will have to establish a social policy on this," he says.[17]

Already, five states offer LMS as an option to more than 90% of their residential customers and 12 more have it available to more than half their subscribers. Despite such penetration, critics bemoan the lack of hard data to demonstrate whether the cost to the telephone companies of metering and billing is actually less than the savings gained and whether measured service in truth saves poorer consumers money.

State commissioners report a strong consumer resistance to the notion of counting the minutes spent talking on the telephone. They worry about the social impact on people confined to their homes such as the elderly and the handicapped. Says Florida commissioner Susan Leisner, "People ought to know what their phone bill will be. There is no way they can do that with LMS."[18]

Just how politically explosive the issue of rising telephone rates will become is unclear. Most consumers remain unaware of the impact of divestiture, competition and deregulation. Some analysts expect an outpouring of rage and confusion. Certainly, there is discomfort among congressmen in Washington, D.C.

Others dismiss the possibility of a major, cohesive consumerist assault on federal and state politicians, pointing out that the totals involved are too small—roughly equivalent to the costs of a tank of gasoline—to generate the kind of outcry that accompanied huge hikes in the price of oil during the 1970s.

Certainly it is true that the totals are not astronomical. For while the local-service portion of the bill will surely increase, the overall bill for many residential consumers may not, due to lower long-distance rates. Says Selwyn, "We won't see a doubling or tripling of the total residential bill. That is completely false."[19]

Professor Trebing of Michigan State adds, "All of this should be kept in perspective. Even if the local rate goes up 100% from an average of $10 a month to $20, that is inconsequential when you compare it with what has happened to natural gas rates recently."[20]

For business services, analysts point out that if rates are set too high, they are likely either to stimulate competition—which would drive prices downward again—or encourage businesses increasingly to build their own telecommunications capability. State commissions are already traumatized by the specter of big corporations such as Citibank—whose annual telephone bill hovers around $160 million—withdrawing from the system and building its own independent systems.

Citibank has purchased two transponders on the Westar communications satellite to exert more control over its costs and to ensure its telecommunications future. The company might even become a common carrier when it leases space on those transponders to other customers.

HOME PHONES GO HIGH-TECH

For consumers who for years have rented a plain black phone with a rotary dial, the futuristic era of razzle-dazzle equipment has arrived, and with it has faded the security about which Russell Baker writes so poignantly. After divestiture, the pace of change that began under FCC deregulation will accelerate, and consumers will face new ways of purchasing and using telephone products. Says Randall L. Tobias, president of the American Bell consumer products group of Western Electric, "We're taking the business we're in today, which the consumer understands as providing residence telephone sets, to a business that meets people's overall information and communication needs."[21]

To that end, consumers will confront some of the following changes.

The Decision to Buy or Lease

Although consumers have been allowed to own their own phones since 1977, few took advantage of the opportunity until AT&T began to promote ownership. Sales ballooned that year, because for most people, the economics of ownership made sense. Leasing costs from $1 to $4 a month, so it takes only one year to cover the cost of buying lower and moderate-priced telephones, and two to three to buy top-of-the-line equipment.

Consumers are also allowed in most states to do their own wiring, thereby saving up to $40 in installation and monthly charges for the wiring of extension phones. Experts say it isn't very difficult. The phone company supplies instructions and wires are color-coded.

The tradeoff, of course, is that owners will be responsible for repairs of phones they own, and for any problems that develop in the wiring. For those who wish to continue leasing, the option will be available from AT&T. After divestiture, the local phone companies will be able to sell, but not lease, equipment.

Widespread Availability of Telephone Equipment from Increasing Numbers of Manufacturers

In anticipation of a colossal burst of business, telephone suppliers are proliferating, and they are wooing consumers with products that range from imported $7.50 throwaway phones to $400 models that feature AM/FM radios and stereo cassette players, plus alarm, toll-call timer and a monitor speaker for hands-free talking. The reason: of the nation's 140 million telephones, only about 5 percent have been purchased.

Some telephone makers predict that phones will soon outstrip stereos, home computers and videocassette records as the fastest-growing consumer electronic product. Besides such traditional suppliers as AT&T, GTE and International Telephone and Telegraph, companies such as General Electric, Tandy, Warner Communications, and a host of foreign firms have jumped into the fray. As many as 17,000 retail stores now sell telephones, including Sears, Radio Shack, the Public Phone Store, catalogue discount stores and corner drugstores.

The FCC Warns Caveat Emptor

"Let the buyer beware," says the FCC to those who buy a one-piece, low-cost, throwaway telephone. To quote an FCC spokesperson, "The FCC only protects the telephone network. It doesn't protect consumers when they buy equipment. When you are no longer in the arms of Mother Bell, quality is not assured."[22]

Increased Sophistication of Equipment

Advances in microelectronic technology have led to smarter telephones, offering residential consumers some of the same conveniences that have intrigued business. For example, speed dialing, call forwarding, call holding (while a caller is serenaded with music), and automatic redialing are all readily available. AT&T's $350 Genesis permits automatic redialing of busy numbers and has an alarm clock and an electronic notebook to remind its owner of important appointments. All this is displayed on a screen that also shows the number dialed, the time of day, the date, and the length of a call.

Far more exotic are home-communications/control centers that use phones to program appliances and lights to turn off and on at prearranged times. These systems also monitor homes for burglary, fire, or utility failure and automatically dial police or fire stations in case of emergency. A nifty variation on that theme is AT&T's medical-alert module, a portable, pocket-sized unit the size of a fat pen, that has a button one can push to summon help in case of a bad fall or illness.

If microelectronic wizardry doesn't captivate the consumer, snobbism is an alternative: designer phones by Geoffrey Beene and Pierre Cardin are also available.

Multiple Billing and the Use of More Than One Carrier

Telephone customers could conceivably receive three separate monthly bills—for equipment rental, local phone service, and long-distance service. AT&T will lease all telephones, while local telephone companies will provide local service. Beginning in 1984, consumers will be asked which long-distance carrier they want to carry their calls. It's possible, however, that AT&T and the other long-distance carriers may farm out all billing to the local companies, in which case, one bill will detail these separate costs.

Changes in Long-distance Calling

After divestiture, consumers will use long-distance carriers not only to call out-of-state but also to make many calls within their states. Because the local telephone companies will be prohibited from routing all calls over the AT&T network, customers will be asked which carrier they wish to use. If a consumer doesn't select one over another, he will dial a code each time he calls that will hook him into AT&T long lines, Sprint, MCI, or other competitors. Right now, that requires dialing ten or more extra numbers. But in the future, connections will be made with four digits or less. Quality of long-distance connections—currently a problem—should improve.

BUSINESS LOOKS TO A DEREGULATED FUTURE

Businessmen say they won't judge divestiture a success unless the local telephone companies take the initiative and provide the services and attention they want.

Says one telecommunications manager with a California company, "We're not sure what is going to happen. The local company may react aggressively in a greater or lesser degree."[23] Whether Pacific Telephone & Telegraph, the financially weakest of the 22 operating companies, will demonstrate the kind of innovative management this California businessman wants is an open question in his mind.

Businessmen praise Southern New England Telephone of New Haven,

Connecticut, as a model of how their local company should react. SNET, as it is known, jumped the gun on the wholly-owned operating companies when it was allowed by the FCC and the court administering the antitrust settlement to enter unregulated markets in 1983, a year before divestiture. The reason: AT&T owns only a minority 24 percent of the company's stock.

SNET lost no time in establishing its image as a lean, tough competitor, unencumbered by its regulated-utility past. The company announced formation of a new subsidiary, Sonecor Systems Division, on January 1, 1983, to sell a wide range of advanced communications equipment, much of it manufactured by AT&T competitors such as Northern Telecom, Nippon Electric, Mitel, TIE Communications, and GTE.

Despite a slimmed-down profile featuring a reduction of at least 1,000 managers from the year before, SNET announced additional new services—a consulting arm to advise customers on their telecommunications needs, a credit subsidiary to help finance equipment, and four retail stores staffed by consultants capable of designing advanced communications systems for the small business.

The company also branched out beyond its Connecticut borders, serving notice that it intends to compete fiercely with both its parent and sibling companies. For example, the company bid to install private telephone systems at the University of Pittsburgh, Stanford, and New York University.

Even with all that expansion, SNET did not ignore regulated telephone services. It filed for a license to set up a digital termination service, a new microwave radio system that will greatly expand its ability to carry high-speed computer data. The company also applied for rights to install cellular radio technology in Connecticut to meet anticipated demand for car telephones.

The other new unleashed competitor in 1983 was AT&T's unregulated subsidiary, which has tried to position itself as a more effective and formidable competitor than AT&T has been in the past. Says Archie J. McGill, former president of the subsidiary's advanced information systems division, "(In the past) the constraints of what we could do, when and how were very severe. The customer will now benefit greatly, because deregulation is permitting us to solve our customers' problems wherever they take us."[24]

AT&T's strategy is to increase productivity of the white-collar worker by beefing up office automation. Says McGill, "We intend to commingle video, sensor and data processing, to significantly decrease the paperwork burden. Say you have a memo and call it up on a terminal display. You can then send it to me and I can respond by voice. We can also eliminate pink calling slips by voice storing. We can automate a company phone book and mail system."[25]

This aggressiveness is a change from the past. Says International Resource Development's Kenneth Bosomworth, "Even though AT&T is the dominant supplier of business in telecommunications, it has not been the driving force in terms of offering new services and products. AT&T in general has been only reacting, and in some cases it failed to react. The pace of events and introduction of new products has been out of AT&T's control for a long time."[26]

Only time will tell whether the subsidiary will evolve into either the profitable and successful information-systems company AT&T so fervently wants, or an industrial disaster. The new company started operations in 1983 with a huge staff, few products and a crushing overhead. Yet no one, especially competitors, is willing to write off the potential impact of a company with such enormous financial, research and manufacturing muscle.

A NEW COMPLEXITY FOR BUSINESS

As competition heats up as a result of divestiture, the job of managing a corporation's telecommunications system will be even more radically revamped. In the past, the position was often held by an ex-Bell System veteran whose main contribution was contacts at Ma Bell to help solve stubborn problems.

The post-divestiture position will require a far more sophisticated approach. Says Dale Cutnick, research chief of Yankee Group, "Telecommunications managers will have to go from being pole climbers to businessmen. They will have to get up to speed to understand what all this is about. That will require knowledge of cost accounting, management of business communications, figuring out traffic patterns."[27]

To that end, graduate schools will offer programs to train students for the new complex world of telecommunications. Michigan State and Colorado, for example, now offer degrees in this field.

The increased sophistication of telecommunications will lead to other trends.

More Business Decisions Based on Telecommunications Costs

In the past, businesses paid little heed to communications costs when it came to making decisions about where to put people and plants. All that is likely to change.

Says Bosomworth, "Telecommunications will become a more important part of the business activity of many companies. It means that companies with remote locations are going to find communications relatively more expensive than locations in major metropolitan areas. That could become a matter of some concern to a company, say an airline, which has typically put reservation centers in remote areas. If telecommunications get 20 percent more or less expensive, that could become the controlling issue of where such facilities are located."[28]

More Private Networks

Predicts Cutnick, "In the next few years we will see feverish activity for building private networks that give the user better cost. The simplest kind will be owning switching equipment but not transmission facilities."[29]

Cutnick predicts that by the mid to late 1980s, most of the top *Fortune 500* industrial companies will operate their own private networks. Since the operating companies will still provide transmission, this will not cause them to lose business. In fact, if they sell switching equipment, they may benefit. He believes that only the biggest companies with the most demanding communications needs such as Citibank are likely to buy their own transmission facilities capable of bypassing the operating companies.

A Bonanza for Telecommunications Consultants

Firms are inundated by requests to study the communications network as a corporate asset. This involves evaluating a company's alternatives, plans, suppliers, and strategies. Since no one vendor offers a complete networking solution, equipment must be evaluated and then pieced together.

Rising Telecommunications Costs Offset by Increased Efficiency and Productivity

Businesses can expect to spend more on communications because they will be accomplishing more. For example, companies like Satellite Business Systems and American Satellite Corporation can link remote computer centers or arrange videoconferences for far-flung executives.

Both AT&T and International Business Machines have announced sophisticated enhanced network services to provide universal data communications by translating automatically between different makes of computers. Such systems will allow a manufacturer to automate his entire ordering, billing and accounting by integrating his computers with those of his customers, suppliers, and bank.

For nearly every type of business, a communications system can be designed to reduce paperwork and delay. For professionals such as doctors and lawyers, there are systems to bill faster. For bank tellers, there are computer terminals with phones linked to alarm systems. Investment bankers can design systems that expedite brokerage orders. Insurance companies can discover ways to handle the huge amounts of data they struggle with daily.

Overall, divestiture presents opportunities to work better, smarter, and faster. And while most businesses do not understand how it will all sort out, they believe that over the long run it will provide them with better control over their fortunes.

NOTES

1. Telephone interview with Robert W. Nichols on May 4, 1983.

2. Telephone interview with Professor Harry M. Trebing on May 4, 1983.

3. Telephone interview with Lee Selwyn on May 6, 1983.

4. Telephone interview with Professor Harry M. Trebing on May 4, 1983.

5. Telephone interview with Robert W. Nichols on May 4, 1983.

6. Telephone interview with Kenneth Bosomworth on May 5, 1983.

7. Telephone interview with Robert Bennis on May 2, 1983.

8. Telephone interview with Robert Bennis on May 2, 1983.

9. Russell Baker, "Sunday Observer" column, *New York Times*, January 3, 1983.

10. Telephone interview with Susan W. Leisner on May 3, 1983.

11. Telephone interview with Robert W. Nichols on May 4, 1983.

12. Telephone interview with Robert W. Nichols on May 4, 1983.

13. Telephone interview with Lee Selwyn on May 6, 1983.

14. Telephone interview with Lee Selwyn on May 6, 1983.

15. Letter from Lewis Perl to the *FCC Communications Daily, Telephone News,* and *Telecommunications Reports* on January 5, 1983 in which he describes testimony he submitted in the AT&T case.

16. Telephone interview with Neil Swift on May 5, 1983.

17. Telephone interview with Neil Swift on May 5, 1983.

18. Telephone interview with Susan Leisner on May 3, 1983.

19. Telephone interview with Lee Selwyn on May 6, 1983.

20. Telephone interview with Professor Trebing on May 4, 1983.

21. In person interview with Randall L. Tobias at American Bell headquarters on February 16, 1983.

22. Telephone interview with William von Alven on May 5, 1983.

23. Telephone interview with Robert Hynes, Telecommunications Manager, Times-Mirror Company on February 22, 1983.

24. In person interview with Archie J. McGill at American Bell headquarters on February 22, 1983.

25. In person interview with Archie J. McGill at American Bell headquarters on February 22, 1983.

26. Telephone interview with Kenneth Bosomworth on May 5, 1983.

27. Telephone interview with Dale Cutnick on May 6, 1983.

28. Telephone interview with Kenneth Bosomworth on May 5, 1983.

29. Telephone interview with Dale Cutnick on May 6, 1983.

REFERENCES

Baker, Russell. January 3, 1983. "Sunday Observer" Column, *New York Times.*

Bell Labs. 1982. *Facts About Bell Labs.* Short Hills, New Jersey, Bell Laboratories.

Bennis, Robert. May 2, 1983. Telephone interview with Robert Bennis, Manager, Communications Systems, Westinghouse Electric Company, New York; conducted by Linda Grant.

Bosomworth, Kenneth. May 5, 1983. Telephone interview with Kenneth Bosomworth, President, International Resource Development, Inc., Stamford, Connecticut; conducted by Linda Grant.

Braun, Ernest and MacDonald, Stuart. 1978. *Revolution in Miniature, The History and Impact of Semiconductor Electronics.* Cambridge, Cambridge University Press.

Brock, Gerald W. 1981. *The Telecommunications Industry.* Cambridge, Harvard University Press.

Brooks, John. 1976. *Telephone.* New York, Harper & Row.

Chip Wars: The Japanese Threat. *Business Week.* Number 2791, May 23, 1983.

Cutnik, Dale. May 6, 1983. Telephone Interview with Dale Cutnik, Research Chief, Yankee Group, Cambridge, Massachusetts; conducted by Linda Grant.

Danielian, N.R. 1939. *A.T.&T.: The Story of Industrial Conquest.* New York, The Vanguard Press.

Federal Communications Commission. 1939. *Final Report-Investigation of the Telephone Industry in the United States.* Washington, D.C., Government Printing Office.

Federal Communications Commission. 1938. *Proposed Report-Telephone Investigation* (known as the *Walker Report*). Washington, D.C., Government Printing Office.

How Government Cases Get Selected. *American Bar Association Anti-Trust Journal.* Spring 1977.

Hynes, Robert. February 22, 1983. Telephone interview with Robert Hynes, Telecommunications Manager, Times-Mirror Company; conducted by Linda Grant.

Kahn, A. E. and Zielinsksi, C. A. New Rate Structures in Communications. *Public Utilities Fortnightly.* March 25,1976.

Kahn, A. E. and Zielinski, C. A. Proper Objectives in Telephone Rate Restructuring. *Public Utilities Fortnightly.* April 8, 1976.

Kohlmeir, Louis M., Jr. 1969. *The Regulators.* New York, Harper & Row.

Leisner, Susan W. May 3, 1983. Telephone interview with Susan W. Leisner, Commissioner, Florida State Public Service Commission; conducted by Linda Grant.

McGill, Archie J. February 22, 1983. In person interview with Archie J. McGill, former president, Advanced Information Systems Division, American Bell, Morristown, New Jersey; conducted by Linda Grant.

Nichols, Robert W. May 4, 1983. Telephone interview with Robert W. Nichols, Legislative and Regulatory Counsel, Consumers Union, Washington, D.C.; conducted by Linda Grant.

Noam, Eli M. Toward an Integrated Communications Market: Overcoming the Local Monopoly of Cable Television. *Federal Communications Law Journal.* Volume 34, Number 2. Spring 1982.

Page, Arthur W. 1941. *The Bell Telephone System.* New York, Harper & Brothers.

Perl, Lewis. January 5, 1983. *Letter* from Lewis Perl, Senior Vice-President, National Economics Research Associates, Inc., New York, to the *FCC Communications Daily, Telephony News* and *Telecommunications Reports.*

Pool, Ithiel de Sola. 1983. *Forecasting the Telephone: A Retrospective Assessment.* Norward, New Jersey, Ablex Publishing Corporation.

Pool, Ithiel de Sola. 1983. *Technologies of Freedom.* Cambridge, Harvard University Press.

President's Task Force on Communications Policy. 1968. *Final Report.* Washington, D.C., Government Printing Office.

Selwyn, Lee. May 6, 1983. Telephone interview with Lee Selwyn, President, Economics & Technology, Inc., Cambridge, Massachusetts; conducted by Linda Grant.

Smith, Adam. 1966. *Theory of Moral Sentiments.* New York, A.M. Kelley.

Swift, Neil. February 16, 1983. Telephone interview with Neil Swift, Director, Communications Division, New York State Public Service Commission; conducted by Linda Grant.

Telecommunications Reports. Volume 49, Number 25, June 27, 1983.

Tobias, Randall L. February 16, 1983. In person interview with Randall L. Tobias, President, Consumer Products Group, Western Electric, Morristown New Jersey; conducted by Linda Grant.

Trebing, Harry M. May 4, 1983. Telephone interview with Professor Harry M. Trebing, Director, Institute of Public Utilities, Michigan State University; conducted by Linda Grant.

Report on Consent Decree Program of the Department of Justice. Washington, D.C., Government Printing Office. United States, House of Representatives, Anti-Trust Subcommittee of the Committee of the Judiciary. 1959.

Wall Street Journal. May 12, 1983, page 27.

INDEX

ABOUT THE EDITOR AND CONTRIBUTORS

Robert W. Crandall is associated with the Brookings Institution and was economic assistant to Federal Communications Commissioner Glen O. Robinson during a portion of the pendency of *U.S. v. AT&T*.

Henry Geller is the director of the Duke University Center for Public Policy Research in Washington, D.C. He served as Assistant Secretary of Commerce for telecommunications during the Carter administration and was general counsel at the Federal Communications Commission.

Linda Grant is the New York Financial Bureau Chief for the *Los Angeles Times*. In her 20-year journalism career, she has also worked for the *Saturday Evening Post*, *Newsweek*, and *Fortune* magazines. She won an Overseas Press Club award in 1968 for reporting from Vietnam and a Gerald Loeb Award for distinguished business journalism in 1982.

Arthur M. Hill, II is manager of business communications marketing for Comsat General. Formerly with Cardiff Publishing and Time-Life News Service, he reported on communications issues and events surrounding the divestiture.

Charles L. Jackson is a Washington consultant and an adjunct professor at Duke University. He has served as staff engineer to the House Telecommunications Subcommittee and prior to that as special assistant to the chief of the Common Carrier Bureau at the Federal Communications Commission (FCC) and as an assistant to an FCC commissioner.

Bruce M. Owen is associated with the firm Owen, Greenhalgh & Myslinski and was chief economist of the antitrust division of the Federal Communications Commission during the period directly preceding the trial of *U.S. v. AT&T*. He was involved in various ways in the decision to file the lawsuit, and was a witness for the government at trial.

Ithiel de Sola Pool is a professor at Massachusetts Institute of Technology and directs the university's research program on communications policy. Dr. Pool is the author of numerous books and articles dealing with communications.

Harry M. Shooshan, III is a Washington consultant and communications lawyer. He is also an adjunct professor at Georgetown University Law Center. For six years, he headed the staff of the Telecommunications Subcommittee in the U.S. House of Representatives and was responsible for the first legislative efforts to deregulate telecommunications and to restructure the Bell System. He participated in the settlement of *U.S. v. AT&T* at the request of Judge Greene. He is also president of the Institute for Information Policy.

Richard E. Wiley is a partner in the Washington, D.C. law firm of Wiley, Johnson & Rein. He is a former chairman of the Federal Communications Commission.

Charles A. Zielinski is a partner in the law firm of Wald, Harkrader & Ross, Washington, D.C. He served as chairman of the New York State Public Service Commission and worked for a number of years prior to that at the Federal Communications Commission.